SEWING TIPS & TRADE SECRETS

SEWING TIPS &
TRADE SECRETS

6464
82

The Taunton Press

Cover photo: Robert Marsala
Designer/Layout Artist: Lynne Phillips

Typeface: Goudy
Paper: S. D. Warren, Somerset Matte, 70 lb.
Printer: Quebecor Printing, Kingsport, Tennessee

Taunton
BOOKS & VIDEOS
for fellow enthusiasts

First printing: 1996
Printed in the United States of America

A THREADS Book

THREADS magazine® is a trademark of The Taunton Press, Inc.
registered in the U.S. Patent and Trademark Office.

The Taunton Press, 63 South Main Street, Box 5506,
Newtown, CT 06470-5506

Library of Congress Cataloging-in-Publication Data

Sewing tips & trade secrets.
        p. cm.
    "Brings together the best information from the Tips and Basics
    columns of Threads magazine" — Introd.
    Includes index.
    ISBN 1-56158-109-7
    1. Sewing.   2. Machine sewing.   I. Threads magazine.
TT705.S474 1996
646.4—dc20   95-47568
                        CIP

CONTENTS

INTRODUCTION

Have you ever wished you could sit at the side of a more experienced sewer so you could pick up the tricks she's learned over the years? With Sewing Tips & Trade Secrets you can sit with many sewers who have found better ways to accomplish sewing tasks.

This book brings together the best information from the Tips and Basics columns of Threads magazine. The Tips column is a forum for readers to share the methods that they've discovered, and the Basics column provides background information about sewing terms and procedures. Thus in this book you'll find not only the right way, but also a better way!

Threads readers are tremendously creative and resourceful—for almost any sewing task, they have figured out new approaches to problems every sewer faces. So whether you are a novice or an experienced sewer yourself, you are sure to find suggestions that will help make your sewing more efficient and more professional.

—Mary Galpin Barnes, editor

Chapter 1

PATTERNS

TWO PATTERN-REINFORCING IDEAS

The first time you use a pattern, make holes at the ends of the darts, and at any other internal point you need to mark (like pocket ends), then reinforce the holes with those little round stick-on reinforcements designed for the paper in loose-leaf binders (available at stationery stores). Each time you use the pattern, you can safely and easily mark through the holes with chalk.
—*Sherry Brown, Brooksville, FL*

Before you cut out a new pattern, tape around all the sharp curves, corners, and along long straight seams with clear cellophane tape. This will prevent these areas from ripping and will keep the edges stiff so they're easy to follow as you cut or trace around the pattern.
—*Sue Weiner, Spring Hill, FL*

PINLESS PATTERN CUTTING

To eliminate the distortion that pins cause when you're securing paper patterns to layered fabrics, especially on small pattern pieces, you can use self-adhesive reinforcing rings from a stationery store instead. Position each ring half on the pattern and half on the fabric wherever you want to secure them together. Because the rings are paper you can cut right through them, and because they're low-tack, they'll pull off the fabric or the pattern without leaving a residue. You don't usually need to remove them because the fabric they're sticking to is scrap, and they won't hurt the pattern. I also use the rings to keep track of the different size needles I'll need for a single project. I write the number on a ring and use it to stick each needle on the front of the machine temporarily.
—*Marjorie Dequincy, Sacramento, CA*

REPRODUCING PATTERNS

Patterns are reproduced for a variety of reasons: You may need an entire front or back pattern, rather than a half; a favorite commercial pattern tissue might have become worn from repeated use; or perhaps you're modifying the pattern. Here is the method used by patternmaker Linda Faiola:

Start with a good *tracing surface* that can withstand a few pinholes. Faiola's movable patternmaking table is a 36-in.-wide hollow-core door, which is very light and easy to move and store, set up on shelving at a comfortable height.

You will also need a *needlepoint tracing wheel* (available from mail-order notions suppliers), which has needle-sharp tips that leave tiny holes in the paper when rolled over the pattern; and a roll of *white paper* to trace the pattern to. (Pencil lines are difficult to see on brown pa-

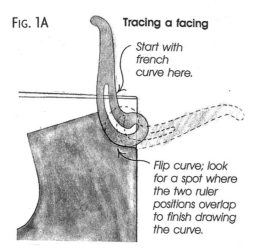

FIG. 1A

Tracing a facing

Start with french curve here.

Flip curve; look for a spot where the two ruler positions overlap to finish drawing the curve.

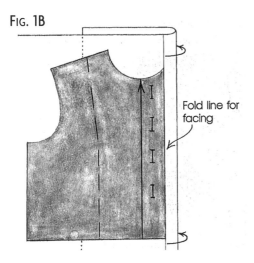

FIG. 1B

Fold line for facing

per.) Flip-chart paper is good; you can find it at art-supply stores.

Place the tissue pattern over the white paper, smoothing the tissue. Tack the pattern down to hold it in place. Roll the needlepoint tracing wheel over the markings that you want to transfer. Remove the tissue pattern; the pinpoint holes, which are likely to be wobbly, are your guides for drawing the pattern lines with rulers and a pencil. The rulers Faiola recommends are an 18-in. C-Thru, a plastic French curve (see Fig. 1A), and a metal yardstick.

For efficient tracing and drawing, trace the stitching lines, not cutting lines. Mark straight lines, including straight-sided darts, at their ends with an X and use a ruler to draw in the final pattern lines. Always include the grainline, which determines the way the garment will hang. *Any line drawn parallel to the grainline, like the center front, also indicates the fabric grain.*

Check matching seamlines for accuracy, then add seam allowances, which can be any width appropriate to the fabric and seam finish.

To draw an entire pattern from a half, start with a straight vertical line in the center of a piece of pattern paper large enough to accommodate the entire front, for example. If you are reproducing a pattern that has a seam allowance at the center, or a lap for buttons, make sure you remove the extra and work with the actual center. Match the center line of the pattern to be transferred over the vertical line. Transfer the

pattern markings and draw the half pattern as discussed. Carefully fold the paper on the center line; a few pins help hold the paper's halves together. Cut out the pattern, being careful not to slice through the fold. Unfold, and you have the entire front.

Use the same technique to add a cut-in facing, shown in Fig. 1B, allowing extra paper for the facing width.

MAKING TAILOR'S TACKS THROUGH PATTERN TISSUE

Use the tip of your needle to make a little slit in the pattern tissue before making a tailor's tack. Then, when you remove the pattern, the tailor's tack slips neatly through the slit without tearing the pattern.

—Mrs. Lee Pecora, Massapequa Park, NY

CLEAN CARDBOARD TEMPLATES

The lightweight, white cardboard used in packaging T-shirts and other clothing is great for making templates for pockets, flaps, collars, or design details such as scallops. Because it's white, I can press over it without damaging my fabric. When I'm finished, I slip the template into the pattern envelope, and it's ready to use the next time.

—Natalie Garrity, Baltimore, MD

RESCALING PATTERNS

When you need to rescale a pattern (either up or down), Ann Hyde, director of the Ann Hyde Institute of Designing, suggests you try this: From a reference point on the pattern piece (like the bottom of the center-back or center-front line) draw straight lines to the other points on the pattern edge (Fig. 2). Measure the lines and divide them in half or in quarters as suits your purpose. Connect the dividing marks with lines identical in shape and angle to the original pattern lines, and you have reduced your pattern. Change dart size and location by the same method.

FIG. 2

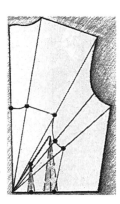

To scale a pattern up, extend the reference lines beyond the edges of the pattern. To turn a quarter-scale pattern into a full-sized one, each line will be increased to four times its original length. Connect the lines as described above.

FREE GRAPH PAPER

When I line storage areas with Con-Tact paper, I peel off the backing carefully because it's marked in 1-in. squares. The backing is perfect for enlarging patterns for small projects, and it's also useful for creating new patterns for small design details, such as collars, cuffs, pockets, facings, and appliqués.
—*Dianne Boate, San Francisco, CA*

A TEMPLATE FOR A STITCHING BOX

Here's an easy way to mark the stitching boxes you need to sew around placket and welt-pocket openings. Cut a template (rotary-cutting is the most accurate way) of just the stitching box from white flannel. The flannel clings to the fashion fabric and is easy to stitch around—no marking required. Store the template with the pattern so you can reuse it.
—*Phyllis Davis, Lakewood, CO*

USING MULTISIZE PATTERNS

I like to use multisize patterns over and over in different sizes for my growing son. Before I lay the pattern tissue on the fabric, I clip the curved areas of the pattern tissue perpendicular to the cutting line and just up to the smallest size as though I were clipping curves in a sewn garment. Where there is a sharp curve, such as in

FIG. 3

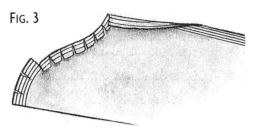

Clip curves to cutting line of smallest size you need, and fold tissue to cutting line.

FIG. 4

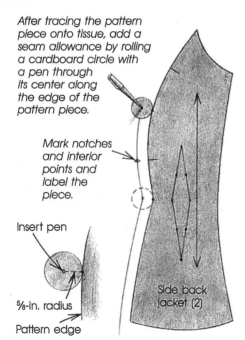

After tracing the pattern piece onto tissue, add a seam allowance by rolling a cardboard circle with a pen through its center along the edge of the pattern piece.

Mark notches and interior points and label the piece.

Insert pen

⅝-in. radius

Pattern edge

Side back jacket (2)

the neck area, I may make six to eight clips. For a raglan or drop-shoulder sleeve, I may make only three or four clips.

I then fold the tissue along the proper cutting line (Fig. 3) and cut out my fabric. When I need to use the pattern for a larger size, all I do is re-fold the pattern along the cutting line for that size. This method will also work for patterns where the garment requires more than one size to fit properly.

—*Shirley Zak, Montara, CA*

TRACING AND MARKING BURDA PATTERNS

I use *Burda* and *Neue Mode* magazines as a source of sewing patterns. To copy pattern pieces without damaging the sheets, I trace the pieces onto a large sheet of rigid plastic (the type used with overhead projectors) with a water-soluble marker. Then I trace the pieces onto blank newsprint or tissue paper. Static electricity holds the plastic to the paper, but in case it does shift, I always start tracing at a corner so I can realign things. The plastic can be used repeatedly.

I prefer to add a seam allowance to the pattern after making adjustments, rather than adding it to the fabric. To do this, you'll need a compass and a piece of thin cardboard. Set the compass to draw a circle with a radius of ⅝ in. or whatever seam allowance you prefer. Then

draw this circle on the cardboard. Cut out the circle and poke a hole in its center. Put your pen tip through the snug-fitting hole, and as you draw around the pattern piece, make sure that the perimeter of the circle touches the pattern's edge exactly, as shown in Fig. 4. When you come to a corner, extend the line past the pattern piece, keeping the same curvature. Mark the corner with a hole in the pattern, and remember to transfer the mark to your fabric. I use a ruler to add large allowances, such as hems. After marking darts, notches, and interior points, I write the name of the garment, the name of the piece, and the number of times to cut it out on each piece.

—*Charlene Pawluck, Charlottetown, Prince Edward Island, Canada*

SHORTENING PATTERNS

The most accurate method sewing instructor Margaret Komives has found for shortening a pattern is to make a fold across the pattern on the lengthen-or-shorten line. To shorten the pattern 1 in., measure 1 in. from one end of the fold and make a mark. Do the same on the other end. Then bring the fold up to the marks and smooth out the entire fold. Tape or pin the tuck in place, as shown in Fig. 5A.

To lengthen the pattern 1 in., slash on the line intended for the alteration. Place a strip of

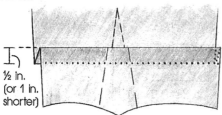

½ in.
(or 1 in.
shorter)

tissue wide enough to accommodate the enlargement under the pattern and tape one side of the pattern to it. Removable tape is useful for this. Measure 1 in. from both ends of the pattern's cut edge and place marks on the tissue. Place the other part of the pattern in such a way that the grainlines are still true and the cut edge is on the marks, as shown in Fig. 5B. Weights are very helpful in holding the pattern while you are doing the taping.

FIG. 5B

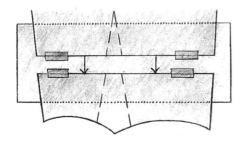

Very often in tucking or spreading a pattern, the lines will be slightly dislocated, especially if they are curved. These lines then must be trued.

LENGTHENING PATTERNS

For fast and easy measuring, I use lined computer paper to lengthen patterns. Attach the paper to your pattern with scraps of fusible interfacing, rather than tape, so you can re-press the pattern.
—Carol Stoner, Denver, CO

USING SCRAP FUSIBLE AS TAPE

A quick and easy method for shortening patterns permanently is to use leftover scraps of fusible interfacing instead of tape. Place the fusible between the overlapped pattern pieces and press lightly. Pressing bonds the fold of the overlap and eliminates the use of tape, which can stick to the sole of the iron if the pattern has to be pressed.
—Mary B. Gibbins, Glenburnie, Ontario, Canada

TAPING PATTERN TISSUE

The perfect tape for tissue-paper pattern alterations is Scotch Brand Post-it Correction and Cover-up Tape, in the 1-in. width. It holds securely if rubbed down a bit and can be moved without tearing and ironed over without shrinking or melting.
—David Coffin, Seymour, CT

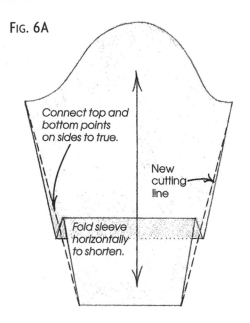

Connect top and bottom points on sides to true.

New cutting line

Fold sleeve horizontally to shorten.

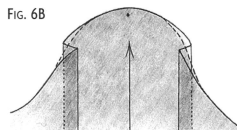

TRUING

Whenever you make adjustments to pattern pieces, such as shortening a sleeve or grading a pattern to a new size, you must redraw the outlines of the piece(s) so that they are smooth, a procedure known as truing. For example, if you have shortened a tapered sleeve by folding the extra length out of the pattern, as shown in Fig. 6A, there will be a jog in the pattern edge. If the sleeve line is straight, use a straightedge to true the cutting line by drawing across the jog from top to bottom of the cutting line.

Truing a line requires a bit of judgment and a few measuring tools or a very good eye. Curved rulers, French curves, and the like are often useful for truing curved lines but some people think that finding just the right curve on the ruler takes longer than judging it by eye. An example of a curved line that was altered and trued is shown in Fig 6B.

VERSATILE PAPER TAPE

Paper surgical tape (such as 3M's Micropore), sold in most drugstores, can be used to mend torn tissue-paper patterns. The lightweight, flexible tape holds paper securely but can be removed easily if you wish to undo the mend. The tape is reusable and comes in ½-in., 1-in., and 2-in. widths.
—*L. D. Pace, Toledo, OR*

MENDING SEWING PATTERNS

Instead of using adhesive tape to mend tears in sewing patterns, I use a strip of Stitch Witchery, sandwiched between the pattern and a piece of the cutaway edge of pattern tissue. The repaired pattern will withstand pressing better than with tape, and it won't get gummy over time.
—*Frankie Leverett, Atlanta, GA*

ALTERING PATTERNS

Rather than cutting and taping pattern pieces to make necessary alterations, I draw new ones using inexpensive waxed paper. I tear off a strip of waxed paper long enough to cover the altered pattern piece. If I need to make the waxed paper wider, I tear off two strips, overlap them lengthwise 3 to 4 in., and bond them by pressing the overlapped area with a hot iron and a press cloth. I lay the waxed paper over the pattern piece and trace the altered piece, using a permanent marking pen.
—*Barbara Burnett, Ft. Worth, TX*

THE FITTING MUSLIN

Making a muslin refers to the process of cutting, sewing, and fitting a test garment, usually in an inexpensive fabric such as muslin. After basting the seams, you place the garment on a dress form or on the body inside out. Working from the inside enables you to mark or pin any fitting changes directly on the seam allowances, for quick adjustments and restitching. When you're satisfied with the style and fit of the test garment, you can rip the muslin pieces apart, true the seamlines, and use the muslin pieces as a pattern for the actual garment.

The extra step of making a test garment requires additional sewing time, but it will help solve fitting and style problems before you cut the fashion fabric. Making a muslin is especially helpful when fit is critical, as in a tailored jacket.

DOUBLE-DUTY GARMENT SAMPLES

I used to make up a new pattern style in muslin to check the fit, later using the muslin for pockets. Now, I make my sample out of preshrunk cotton batiste in the same color as the garment-to-be and use it as an underlining. This works well when the dresses are made of lightweight silky polyester material. The lining makes my garments easier to handle and more comfortable to wear.

—Liz Violante, Marco Island, FL

FITTING BY VIDEO

One day as my husband watched me peering into a hand mirror to check the fit of a sleeve in a full-length mirror. he suggested I use a video camera for fitting. Here's how it works: I place the camera on a table (a tripod would work) and set it to automatic focus, then walk in front of the camera and turn slowly, raise my arms, reach forward, and so forth. I review the tape, fitting book in hand. This method allows me, a beginning seamstress, to see exactly what's going on, to make changes, and to compare.

—Susan M. Piernan, Mill Valley, CA

SAFETY PINNING

When pinning layers (fabric, pattern pieces, etc.) together, I find that burying the point of the pin between the layers, as shown in Fig. 7, after the initial pinning makes it easier not to prick myself.

—Mary Hardenbrook, Huntington Beach, CA

SECURE PINS FOR FITTING

We've all heard the "Ouch!" from the fittee when a previously placed pin shifts and pokes. To avoid the ouch and keep pins from escaping, slip a spare barrel-type pierced earring back (the "butterfly" type won't cover the point) over the points of the pins in the most critical places as

FIG. 7

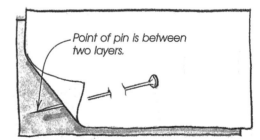

Point of pin is between two layers.

you fit. Most bead shops can sell you a handful of backs if you don't have any lying around. They call them barrel ear nuts.
—*Beverly Stone, Encinitas, CA*

MARKING GRAINLINES

To pull (remove) threads for marking the grainlines on a muslin, try the method used by sewing instructor Suzanne Stern: Pull two adjacent threads, one at a time, since one pulled thread is too hard to see, and three pulled threads will actually allow the fabric to distort. Clip through the selvage, if any, with scissors, then start about 1 in. from the edge by loosening and pulling a thread free with a needle. Hold the inch-long end in one hand and slightly gather the fabric along it (as shown in Fig. 8), a few inches at a time, never pulling hard enough to break the thread as you work toward the opposite edge. Gather the fabric just enough to loosen the thread along its whole length, at which point it should be easy to slide the thread completely out of the fabric. Wind the pulled length around your finger as you pull it out, so it's less likely to break. If it does break at any point, simply pull out the broken length and continue by loosening the remaining end enough to grab. Pull out the adjacent thread in the same way, which should be much easier than pulling the first thread.

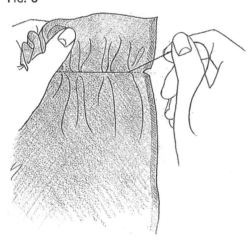

FIG. 8

NO-RESIDUE FABRIC MARKING

When I'm machine-stitching on the right side of a garment and need to follow pattern markings, e.g., buttonholes or the front fly on a pair of pants, I mark the wrong side of the fabric with tracing paper and wheel directly from the pattern. Then I handsew a running stitch directly over the traced markings with contrasting thread to transfer the markings to the right side of the fabric. I use this thread marking as my guide when machine-stitching and simply pull the handsewn threads out when I'm finished. This leaves no unsightly chalk or tracing marks.
—*Susanna Prentiss, Head of Chezzetcook, Nova Scotia, Canada*

PRESERVING PATTERN NOTCHES

When finishing the raw edges of seam allowances that I will press open, I find it frustrating that the serger cuts off the notches I need for matching seams. How to avoid it? I simply fold the notch under and even with the raw edge of the fabric before it reaches the cutting blade. The notches remain intact and visible in the seam when I need them. This works well for both lightweight and heavier-weight fabrics. To eliminate bulk, I trim the notches after stitching the seam.
—*Joanna Wilson, Dover, DE*

MATCHING STRIPES

To help match stripes from piece to piece when laying out patterns, I trace the stripes from the fabric onto the paper pattern with pencil and a straightedge. I erase the lines when I reuse the pattern for another fabric style.
—*Marie Dunn, Withington, Manchester, England*

MATCHING PLAIDS

Here's my method of matching stripes and plaids. Lay the corresponding pieces right sides together. Then turn back the seam allowance on the top piece from ¼ to ⅝ in. Stitch on the turned-back seam allowance next to the fold, as shown in Fig. 9 (⅛ in. away for heavy fabrics). Adjust the fabrics as you sew to line up the stripe or plaid exactly. The seam will lie flat and open and won't pull out, since it is stitched through two layers of fabric. This method also works on curved seams and is always accurate because you're matching right sides.
—*Marguerite F. Connors, Danvers, MA*

MATCHING PLAIDS IN SLEEVES

In order to match plaids accurately in a set-in sleeve, I first cut the sleeve from muslin. I assemble the muslin sleeve in the usual way, and machine-baste it into the bodice (which has been cut and assembled in the fashion fabric).

With the muslin sleeve set into the armhole, I carefully mark it at the lines where the bodice plaids join the sleeve. I remove the "pattern" sleeve, place it on the uncut fashion fabric with the markings matching, and cut a perfect sleeve.
—*Mary Hardenbrook, Huntington Beach, CA*

THE ARMSCYE

Armscye (sounds like arms-eye), another word for armhole, is the opening in a garment for a sleeve. According to sewing author Claire B. Shaeffer, armscye is a term that's traditionally been used in tailoring and in the clothing industry more than by the home sewer.

The shape of an armscye usually curves more deeply into the garment front than back to accommodate the forward motion of the arm. On a pattern piece, the front is always marked with one notch and the back with two, which helps in identifying a garment section whose pattern piece has been removed.

For a basic fitted bodice, the depth of the armscye should fall approximately ½ in. below the armpit. To determine this point, hold a 1-in.-wide ruler horizontally under the arm. Mark the bottom of the ruler on the bodice, remove the ruler, and mark the underarm depth ½ in. higher.

For a sleeveless garment, you'll want the base of the armhole to be from ⅜ to ½ in. higher than for the basic fitted bodice. In a tailored

FIG. 9

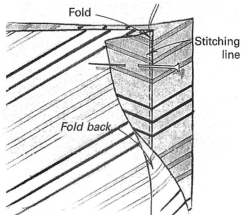

Fold upper seam allowance back almost to stitching line, and stitch along fold to match plaids exactly.

garment, the depth of the armscye usually falls about ⅜ to ½ in. lower than for the basic fitted bodice, and for a coat, ¾ in. lower.

To check the alignment of an armscye, view the garment on the body from all sides. The armscye seam should appear to be straight when viewed from the top of the shoulder. It should also appear to be straight when viewed from the front and back, and more or less parallel to the garment center.

REFERENCE LABELS

To keep track of what pattern(s) I use to make my garments, I make labels from satin ribbon, using the alphabet embroidery feature on my machine. With a strip of tear-away backing under the ribbon, I sew the first three letters of the pattern company name and the pattern number in contrasting thread. After treating the cut edges with a fray preventive, I attach my "custom reference" to the inside of the garment.
—*Carla H. Johnson, Baltimore, MD*

PIVOTING A DART

Pivoting a dart is a design change that repositions a dart so it starts at a different place on the perimeter of a garment, without changing the apex to which the dart points, or the fit. (This is not the same as moving a dart, which is a fitting adjustment that is required when the bust point or other apex has been relocated.) Pivoting is often used to shift a bust dart from a horizontal to a vertical position without changing any aspect of the garment's fit.

To pivot a bust dart, first redraw the dart legs as shown in step 1 in Fig. 10 so they reach the bust point. Lay the pattern over another sheet of paper larger than the pattern, put both layers on a pinnable surface, and pin straight down through the bust point so that the pattern pivots around it. Draw a line from where you want the new dart located on the pattern edge to the bust point (step 2), then cut away the inside of the existing dart along the new legs, leaving a tiny bit of paper uncut below the pin.

Next, cut along the new dart placement line from the outside edge almost to the bust point, then shift the pattern piece from the old to the new dart by closing the original dart. This auto-

FIG. 10

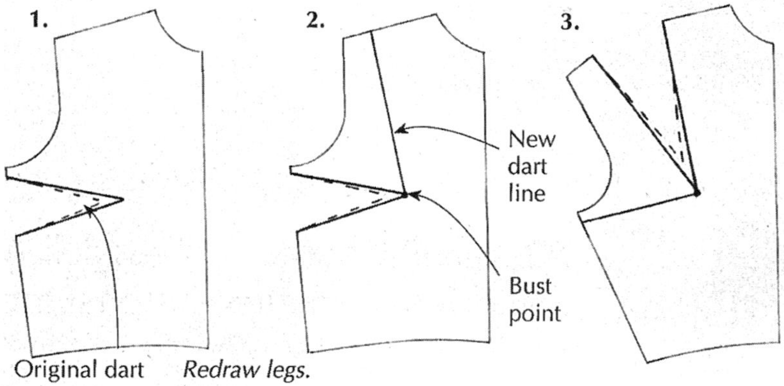

1. **2.** **3.**

New dart line

Bust point

Original dart   *Redraw legs.*

matically opens a new, identically sized dart at the slash of the new placement line, as shown in step 3. Tape the old dart closed and the opening at the new dart to the paper underneath, then shorten the new legs so that they're the same distance from the bust point as the old legs were. Remove the pin and fold the new dart closed to one side, as you'll press it on the garment: then trim the fold along the seam-allowance edge to shape the new dart end.

BEFORE YOU FOLD A SEWING PATTERN

Here's a simple idea that's saved me a lot of time and shuffling when I'm looking for pattern parts: Just make sure you fold each pattern piece so that the style number and the name or number of the piece are visible. This makes it easy to pull out just a collar or pocket when experimenting with combined patterns, without having to unfold each piece.
—*Elizabeth Rydman-Harris, Santa Fe, NM*

ORGANIZING PAPER PATTERNS

To create some order out of the chaos of my unruly collection of *Burda* pattern tracings, I decided to box and arrange them in categories. At my local comic-book store, I bought a package of 7-in. by 10-in. plastic comic-book sleeves and an assortment of storage boxes. Since the boxes come in various lengths, I was able to buy just the size box I needed for each category. Inside each sleeve, I put the pattern, the original photo of the garment, a master sheet containing all pertinent measurements, and a swatch of fabric.
—*Anne Ruby, Brookline, MA*

STORING PATTERNS

I place small patterns that fit comfortably in their own envelopes into quart-size zip-closing plastic bags. Larger patterns make the bags bulge and slip. For those I use 9x12 paper envelopes recycled from our daily mail. I paste the front of the pattern envelope on the left side of the front of the envelope, and on the right side I paste the back of the pattern envelope. Sometimes they require a little trimming, but these envelopes fit perfectly in a home filing cabinet, where I further identify them with filing labels.

I carefully roll very large patterns, which would need many folds to fit into an envelope, and I slip them into a cardboard paper-towel roll, which I label and place on a storage shelf.
—*Solange Hawkins, Marietta, GA*

WRINKLE-FREE PATTERNS

As a patternmaking student at Oregon School of Arts and Crafts, I've stumbled upon a great solution for storing patterns that eliminates the need to iron them each time they're used. Instead of folding them back into their small envelopes, I roll them up and slip them into cardboard tubes from kitchen and gift wrap.

—*Linda Kuras, Portland, OR*

STIFFER PATTERN PIECES

If you spray tissue-paper sewing patterns with a light coating of starch, then let them dry before putting them away, they'll be a little stiffer and easier to handle next time. (Pressing the patterns when they're damp may tear them.) To avoid folding the pattern pieces, I pack them away in suit boxes.

—*Sherry Brown, Brooksville, FL*

INTERFACING AS PATTERN PAPER

Lightweight, nonwoven, sew-in interfacing is a good substitute for tissue paper or shelf paper when you're tracing or correcting a pattern or making an original pattern by flat pattern drafting. Interfacing is sturdier and lasts longer than tissue paper, but it's still transparent; stores well folded; irons out nicely with a warm, dry iron; and resists tearing, even when traced over with a tracing wheel. You don't need the best quality, so get it in bulk at a discount fabric store.

—*Fredricka Housman, Naples, FL*

NEWSPRINT AS PATTERN PAPER

Newsprint roll ends, which are available at your local newspaper, are a great source of lightweight, extra-wide patternmaking paper. I paid only a $1 deposit to my newspaper to ensure that I would return the cylinder—the paper was free.

—*Deborah C Little, Alva, FL*

PRESERVING PATTERN TISSUES

You can conserve worn tissue-paper patterns or protect new ones and make them easier to use at the same time.

I fuse lightweight, nonwoven, white interfacing to the wrong side of the pattern before I cut the pieces apart. This way I don't have to waste a lot of time and energy cutting the interfacing to an exact shape or risk getting goo on my iron. Since the lightweight interfacing is translucent, the pattern is legible from both sides, and it's also easier to cut accurately. The pattern is rip-resistant and easy to put away unrumpled.

—*Tammy Baran, Orlando, FL*

PRESERVING SEWING PATTERNS

Patterns tend to wear out with repeated use. To slow the wear and tear, I preserve each one with plastic-coated freezer wrap, which you can buy in most grocery stores. Place the pattern pieces face down on the plastic and press with a dry iron set on a silk temperature. Press only the pattern piece; if your iron strays onto the freezer wrap, the plastic will fuse to your iron.

—*Suzan Wiener, Spring Hill, FL*

A BINDER INDEX FOR SEWING PATTERNS

Organizing sewing patterns into categories makes browsing easier. This can be done by photocopying the pattern envelopes and arranging them in a three-ring binder. If you are unable to get double-sided copies of your pattern envelopes, glue or staple the fronts and backs together. Plastic photograph sleeves that fit a three-ring binder, found in stationery stores, are a convenient way to display your copies. Attach any fabrics, notes, or other relevant information to the patterns.

—*Kristine Kadlec, Los Angeles, CA*

REUSABLE SEWING PATTERNS

Wallpaper from the bargain bin at your local wallpaper shop is great for making copies of often-used sewing patterns. The best paper is any light-colored vinylized type that's not embossed or flocked. If you can find a checked paper you can even use the pattern to mark the grain; I've found double rolls for as little as $3. Transfer the pattern with a tracing wheel and mark with a felt pen. To store the pieces, punch a hole at the top of each one, reinforce with gummed rings from a stationery store, and keep complete patterns together with a metal shower-curtain ring so you can hang the patterns on the wall without folding or rolling them.

—*Moyra A. Pepper, Victoria, British Columbia, Canada*

MARKING PATTERN OUTLINES

Tracing tissue patterns onto stiffer paper with a pencil or pen often means losing the thin lines when you cut out the pattern. To create a more visible outline, place the stiff paper pattern over a sheet of scrap paper and go over the edges with a broad-tip high-lighter or felt-tip pen.

—*Rita Jacobson, Fountain Valley, CA*

Chapter 2

TOOLS

THREADING A NEEDLE AND PULLING IT THROUGH

Butler Eez-Thru Floss Threaders, designed to help thread dental floss between teeth and available at the pharmacy, work just as well for threading needles, as shown in Fig. 11, provided the needle's eye is not too tiny.

—*Ilene F. Joyce, Boise, ID*

FISHING FOR THREAD ENDS

Every turn-of-the-century seamstress kept a "fishing line" in her workbox for hiding thread ends and burying snags. This handy device is no more than a needle threaded with twice the needle's length of thread plus 2 in. Knot the ends of the thread separately so they won't slip off the needle. Push the eye of the needle through the fabric from the wrong side at the point of the loose thread, as shown in Fig. 12. Move the needle up so that the eye shows, then slowly pull it back down, leaving a loop of thread on the right side. Push the loose end through the loop, then pull the knotted end of the needle thread to hold the unwanted thread firmly against the needle's eye. Pull the needle out and the loose end will follow, hiding obediently under the fabric.

—*Elaine Middaugh, Brookings, SD*

CUSTOMIZING YOUR TAPE MEASURE

If you've got a few measurements that you use all the time, such as the hem length you like for skirts or the inseam length on finished pants, you can keep a permanent record of them with marks on your tape measure at these lengths. I use a colored marker to make a thin line across the tape and label each one with a short code, like "H" for hem, and "I" for inseam.

—*Lucy Thompson, Livingston, TX*

A THIMBLE ALTERNATIVE

Not everyone is comfortable using the classic metal thimble. The alternative that's worked for me is to use an inexpensive rubber finger cover of the type sold in stationery stores to help in sorting and counting paper. The rubber is typically thicker at the tip than on the sides, offering almost the same protection from needle ends, and the sides of the device provide increased grip, useful for pulling stuck needles through. I prefer the smooth fingers to the ones with texture or little bumps.

—*Dawn Lesley Stewart, Holliston, MA*

FIG. 11

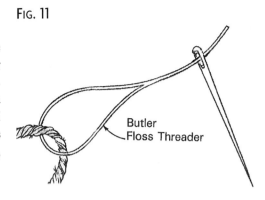

Butler Floss Threader

FIG. 12

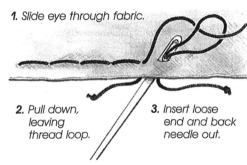

1. Slide eye through fabric.

2. Pull down, leaving thread loop.

3. Insert loose end and back needle out.

FIG. 13

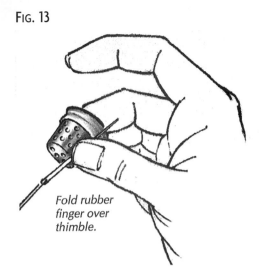

Fold rubber
finger over
thimble.

FIG. 14

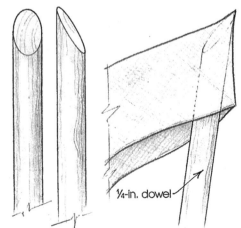

¼-in. dowel

A PUSH-AND-PULL THIMBLE

By lining an oversize metal thimble with a rubber finger cover from the office-supply shop, you can create a double-duty device that makes grabbing needles as easy as pushing them, with no need to reach for or find an extra tool. Turn the excess length of the rubber fingertip over the bottom edge of the metal thimble, as shown in Fig. 13, securing the excess in place and positioning a layer of rubber where you can use it to pinch and pull your needle.

—*Vicki Tatum Stammer, Arlington, TX*

A HOMEMADE POINT TURNER

I made myself a tool for turning points and opening seams that I find superior to anything else I've tried. Starting with a ¼-in. hardwood dowel cut 14 in. long, I used a craft knife to shape the end into a flattened oval, as shown in Fig. 14. After being smoothed with fine sandpaper, the tip is wonderful for turning collar points, and the flattened edge presses the seam open for a crisp, sharp edge.

—*Terry Grant, Ashland, OR*

MECHANICAL-PENCIL POINT TURNER

A good tool for poking out corners, like the points of collars when you're turning them right side out, is a mechanical pencil with the lead retracted. The point is narrow, but not sharp enough to poke through the fabric easily.

—*Edith Frankel, Hannawa Falls, NY*

ELEVENTH FINGER

I've found that the tiny screwdriver for my sewing machine makes an excellent extra finger to hold down and control the edge of an appliqué as I sew it in place with a satin stitch or other decorative machine stitch. It's possible to allow the point of the screwdriver to ride the fabric right up to the foot and under the upturned edge until the last second, when the fabric is firmly between the presser foot and throat plate. You won't sew a finger, and your line of vision is clear.

—*Diane Schultz, St. Paul, MN*

HEMOSTATS AS SEWING AIDS

I keep a pair of surgeon's clamps (hemostats—bought at a local surgical supply store) on my sewing table. Their rounded ends make them

excellent for shaping collar points, and they are handy to use with piping. After sewing piping in a seam, I use my hemostats to hold the piping so I can trim the cord out of the seam allowance, as shown in Fig. 15. To protect the piping from the serrated jaws, put a scrap of fabric between them and the piping. Clamp the piping tightly 2½ in. from the garment's edge to secure the cord, then slide the fabric back and trim ⅝ in. from the cord. When you press the seam open, there's no cord to add bulk.
—*Dale Jenssen, Taos, NM*

HANDY THIRD HAND

Your sewing machine can double as a third hand, or sewing bird, for easier ripping and hand sewing. Put your work under the presser foot—feed dogs and needle up—and drop the foot. If the fabric is fragile or slips, put a wide rubber band between the fabric and the presser foot (Fig. 16). I have a sewing machine with a quick-changing foot system, so I take one of the feet I rarely use and wrap it with a rubber band. I pop it on for lengthy ripping jobs.
—*Marianne Kantor, Bondville, VT*

SODA-CAN BODKIN

Next time you're trying to thread elastic into a casing, reach for a soda can—not for a drink, but for the metal tab on top. Snap the tab off the can and you will have a perfect two-hole handle for attaching the elastic and pulling it through. The smaller hole, which was attached to the can, is slightly jagged, so it's the better one to attach the elastic to. Slip the elastic through the hole and tack near the end. The larger hole is an ideal size and thickness for pulling through gathers. I find this so much better than a safety pin that I've installed a can tab permanently in my sewing kit.
—*Susan Delaney Mech, Plano, TX*

ONE-STEP ELASTIC PULLING AND TUBE TURNING

Here's a quick way to turn a tube or casing and insert elastic at the same time. I use a readily available notion called an Elastic Glide (sold at most notions counters) as the turning device because it's inexpensive and it won't hurt the needle if I happen to hit it while tacking it down. I start by cutting the casing fabric at least 2 in. longer than its finished length. Next, I machine-stitch both the Glide and one end of the elastic to the extra length on the right side

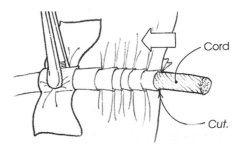

FIG. 15

Cord

Cut.

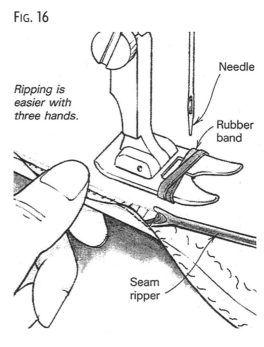

FIG. 16

Ripping is easier with three hands.

Needle

Rubber band

Seam ripper

FIG. 17

FIG. 18

of the unstitched casing, as shown at top in Fig. 17, using a wide, zero-length zigzag bar tack. After stitching the casing closed and trimming the seam allowances to ⅛ in., I clip diagonally across the extra length just above the bar tack to reduce bulk and make turning easier, as shown at bottom in Fig. 17. Now I simply slip the fabric over the Glide, enclosing the elastic as I expose the Glide. Finally, I trim away the excess casing and clip the bar tack so I can reuse the Glide. Of course, this method works perfectly well when you're turning a tube; just leave out the elastic.

—*Toni Toomey, Woodbury, CT*

BUTTONHOLE CHISEL FOR WELT CORNERS

When you're making welt pockets, bound buttonholes, and anything else that requires clipping all the way into a stitched corner, it's often difficult to clip safely as far as you need to with the tips of scissors. A better tool is a buttonhole chisel (which comes with its little companion block of wood), shown in Fig. 18 and available at most notions counters and by mail from the major notions catalogs. Of course, the chisel is perfect for clean, precise openings in buttonholes, but you can also easily position the end of the chisel blade exactly at the corner you need to clip into. Push it through the fabric and your clipping will be perfect. If the blade is too wide for the hole or clipping you need to make, just position the cutting area over the edge of the wooden block. The chisel will cut only as far as the block extends.

—*Mary Jane McClelland, Diamond Bar, CA*

MAKING A CORD GUIDE

If the needle plate on your sewing machine doesn't have a hole through which to thread cord for padding pin tucks and doing cord quilting, you can make your own guide from an ordinary paper clip. Use needle-nosed pliers to pinch the inside loop of the clip to a $\frac{1}{16}$-in. opening (Fig. 19A). Bend the end up enough to allow a heavy cord, such as #3 perle cotton, to pass through. Cut off the larger loop of the clip about $\frac{1}{4}$ in. behind the cord loop.

Tape the clip to the needle plate or bobbin cover with the cord loop facing the needle and centered about $\frac{5}{8}$ in. from the needle hole, as shown in Fig. 19B.

To control the ball of cord with this guide or with the one built into your machine or presser foot, drop it into a small knife-folded paper bag taped to the edge of your sewing-machine table. Thread the cord through the loop and let it self-feed. The tension created by the narrow fold of the bag will be just enough to feed the cord smoothly.

—*Elizabeth Lee Richter, Huntington, CT*

ORGANIZING NOTIONS

To organize thread and small notions, I bought several 4x8 fiberboard panels at a lumber yard and mounted them on a wall in my sewing room. Straight pins stuck into the board hold notions and fashion ideas, while rows of finishing (headless) nails organize spools of thread, bobbins, and lightweight tools. Some lumber companies will cut the panels to specific sizes upon request. These lightweight boards can be nailed or screwed directly through the wall into the wall studs. The scratchy fiber board can be covered with muslin, burlap, or other fabric.

—*Barbara Burnett, Fort Worth, TX*

WALL ORGANIZER

An upholstered wall is a wonderful sewing aid that will also lighten and brighten a small, dark sewing room. First, staple a layer of medium-weight polyester batting directly to the wall or paneling, using a staple gun and medium staples. (The staples leave minimal holes.) Cut a king-sized sheet to cover the batting, leaving enough allowance to turn under the edges. Staple the sheet to the batting. Long quilting pins are ideal for hanging sketches, fabric swatches, notes, etc. You can pin up an entire garment's pieces, along with notions and pattern tissues, preventing wrinkles. Best of all, all the pieces are out of the way until sewing time.

—*Susan Mackenzie, Grants Pass, OR*

FIG. 19A

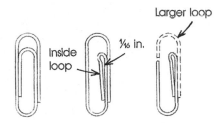

Compress inside loop of a paper clip to $\frac{1}{16}$ in., bend it up slightly, and cut off larger loop $\frac{1}{4}$ in. behind it.

FIG. 19B

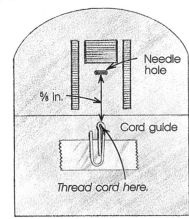

Tape cord guide about $\frac{5}{8}$ in. in front of needle hole.

FIG. 20

Cardboard tube   Dowel

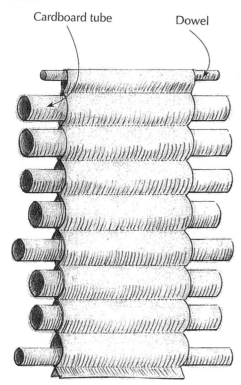

WALL STORAGE FOR ROLLS AND TUBES

There are a lot of materials in the average sewing or quilting work area that can be stored by being rolled up: interfacings, stabilizers, fabric scraps, even patterns you don't want to fold. I've devised a handy storage unit for them that keeps them on the wall out of the way (Fig. 20). You need a long, 12-in. wide scrap of fabric or canvas, a dowel or metal rod about that long, and a few empty cardboard tubes from paper towels. First make a list of the items you need to store, adding to the count to allow for future items. Multiply the number of items by 6 in. to determine the length of fabric you need. You can staystitch the edges of your fabric strip, serge them, or leave them raw. Fold the short ends of the strip together, measure 1½ in. down from the fold, and stitch across, creating a casing for the dowel that will hold the unit to the wall. Then mark off from that stitching 3-in. divisions along the remaining length and stitch across at each mark, making casings for the tubes. If you're using any wrapping paper tubes, mark off 3½-in. divisions for each one and more for any casings for larger rolls. The tubes will make it easy to slip your rolled items into and out of storage once you've hung your roll-holder on the wall. Finish the raw edges at the ends of the strip with simple rolled or folded hems.
—*Dorothy Fusselman, Chagrin Falls, OH*

CLOSET STORAGE ORGANIZERS

A vinyl shoe organizer, hung from a closet rod, is an ideal storage container for scraps of fabrics and other miscellaneous sewing items. The organizer that I have has 18 to 20 individual vertical pockets 9 in. wide by 6 in. deep. I also use a sweater organizer to store flat folded yardage.
—*Judy Zifka, Bend, OR*

TWO SEWING TOOLBOXES

A large fishing-tackle box that has multi-layered trays is ideal for organizing sewing accessories. The small compartments are useful for needles, pins, buttons, and beads. The bottom of the box will hold sewing books, instruction manuals, patterns, and similar items. Fishing-tackle boxes are well balanced and can be left open for easy rummaging. They can also be packed up quickly for taking to classes.
—*Mrs. Mary Ann James, Owego, NY*

To make a tool holder for my sewing equipment, I cleaned up an old toolbox caddy and put a lazy Susan under it so that it could spin to within my reach. The drawers hold fasteners, safety pins, thimbles, seam rippers, tweezers, bobbins, and chalk. I hang my scissors on the outside hooks. The bins are great for tapes and trims, rulers,

and glues. With a twist of the wrist I have all my sewing supplies within reach, and the tool holder takes up little space behind my machine.
—*Jan Scholl, State College, PA*

STORAGE FOR RECYCLED NOTIONS

A beautiful wooden spice rack with fitted glass jars that I found at a garage sale has been reborn in my sewing room as storage for all those tiny items that previously were jumbled in the bottom of a drawer. Buttons can be sorted by color, needles by size and type, and so on. Labels aren't necessary, and the whole thing can be hung in plain sight but out of the way on a wall.
—*Mary E. Green, Toledo, OH*

STORAGE FOR USED BUT STILL-LIVE NEEDLES

When you've used a sewing-machine needle briefly and want to store it for future use, stick it in a scrap of the fabric for which it's appropriate. For example, stick a 100/16 jeans needle into a scrap of denim, or 60/8 sharp into a scrap of silk. This way you can tell at a glance whether used needles are still usable and also what they're to be used for.
—*Jenny Lewis, Portsmouth, NH*

HANDY HANGERS

If you don't have a dress form, you can still enjoy many of its benefits with a few simple tricks for hanging your garments-in-progress. Skirts that need to hang overnight before being hemmed can be suspended from a plain coat hanger on which you've placed four or five large spring clips. These will support the entire waistband more uniformly and more flexibly than a regular pant or skirt hanger. Flared or circular skirts do better hung in the round; an inflated beach ball inserted inside the skirt will do the trick, hung by a piece of string from the blow-up valve. I installed a ceiling hook, of the sort used to hang plants, in a convenient place in my sewing-room ceiling, and hung from it a length of twill tape knotted at intervals into loops. I can hang garments at various heights from the loops and turn them easily to work on or view.
—*Lena M. Wardell, Burlington, Ontario, Canada*

PADDING UP A DRESS FORM

When I am draping for a larger-sized bust than my dress form has, I use shoulder pads to enlarge the bust measurement. I usually use two pads on each side, as shown in Fig. 21. Since you can get shoulder pads in all thicknesses, you can really customize the shape, and the body will always be symmetrical.
—*Marlene Vincent, Flushing, NY*

FIG. 21

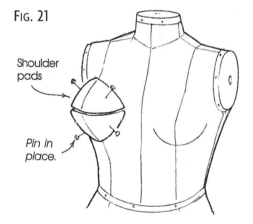

Shoulder pads

Pin in place.

BRA AND SLIP PAD DRESS FORM

When I had to pad my old dress form, I put a well-fitting bra and snug-fitting old nylon slip on the form. The bra provides the correct bust shape as well as defining the correct position of the bustline. I marked my waistline on the slip with a marker pen and slipped it over the form, padding the slip to complete the shape.
—*Marla Zbornik, Rudd, IA*

NEW LIFE FOR MARKING PENS

The water-soluble felt-tip pens popular today, such as Mark-Be-Gone, tend to have a short life even when capped. To extend their life, store them in a resealable plastic bag.
—*Vicki Leavitt Combs, Hughesville, MD*

Here's a tip to extend the life of a water-soluble fabric pen: When it goes dry, pop off the blunt end, put six or seven drops of rubbing alcohol into the barrel, and shake.
—*Tenley Alaimo, Endicott, NY*

WASHABLE MARKERS

I've discovered that the widely available Crayola Washable Markers make wonderful fabric markers; the ink washes out instantly in cold water. The package states that normal launder-ing will remove ink marks from cotton, poly-ester, acrylic, nylon, and their blends. These markers come in colors that work on virtually every shade of fabric except pure black.
—*Blanche Rehling, Millstadt, IL*

SOAP AS TAILOR'S CHALK

I have been saving wedges of soap and using them as tailor's chalk for years. The best soap to use is a hard-water Castile bar, found in most grocery and some health-food stores. It is rec-tangular and wears down to a very thin palm-size piece. Let the wedge dry and harden in the air for about a week. To keep the fine edge sharp, store in the open air, not in a container or plastic. The soap markings are easy to erase with a moist fingertip. This natural soap will not harm delicate silks, antique textiles, or fab-rics requiring dry cleaning.
—*Sandra Lee Wollin, Emerson, NJ*

DRAFTING SUPPLIES FOR SEWERS

I have learned to think of the local drafting and art-supply store as my second notions shop. This store carries inexpensive draftsman's tracing pa-per on 50-yd. rolls, in widths from 12 in. to 48 in. The surface takes pen and pencil equally well. This paper also comes in large-sized pads and is transparent, making copying patterns easy. I also buy a large sheet of mat board to cover my folding cutting board and smooth out the surface. Mat board comes in many colors and sizes from 22 by 30 in. to 40 by 60 in.

Another drafting tool that I find very useful in the sewing room is the flexible curve. My drafting store has them in lengths from 12 to 36 in. The lead core with spring steel inserts lets them hold any shape, and they have a beaded edge against which to run a pen or tracing wheel. (They are too easily marred to use with a rotary cutter, though.) These flexible curves also make excellent pattern weights when used coiled or shaped around a pattern curve.
—*Barbara Nachtigall, Roslindale, MA*

TWO QUICK CUTTING TABLES

If you're pressed for cutting-out space, here's a quick, inexpensive, and easily disassembled solution: Pick up a second adjustable ironing board (asuming you've already got one)—check thrift shops for a second-hand one. Also get one of those folding cardboard cutting boards from the fabric store. Set up the two ironing boards at the same height side by side and about 10 in. apart, but pointing in opposite directions, and use them as a sturdy base for the cutting board. This won't do for really heavy-duty jobs, but it's

quite serviceable for everyday cutting, and it stores in not much more space than you're already using for one ironing board.
—*Juinona J. Porter, New Philadelphia, OH*

To make a cutting board, I buy a 4x8 sheet of building board from the lumber yard. This is a lightweight, porous cardboard about ½ in. thick that pins can easily penetrate. It can be cut to size with a drywall knife. I made mine 30 in. by 60 in., and covered it with a close-fitting cotton cover to keep the edges from being damaged. I put it on top of the adjustable ironing board, so I can work all the way around it; I store the board against the wall when I'm not using it.
—*Eva Braswell, Bloomington, IL*

HOMEMADE SERGER GUIDELINES

My handwoven fabric is not easy to mark with chalk, but I need a precise and very visible guideline to follow when I serge curved shapes on it. I discovered that I could mark the curve with ¹⁄₁₆-in. contour drafting tape, as shown in Fig. 22. It is pliable, pulls off easily, and makes the process go faster. You can find the tape in art or drafting supply stores. I used Letraset Letraline, which comes in a plastic dispenser.
—*M. Lynette Holmes, Littleton, CO*

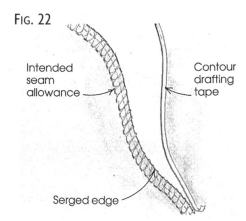

FIG. 22

Intended seam allowance

Contour drafting tape

Serged edge

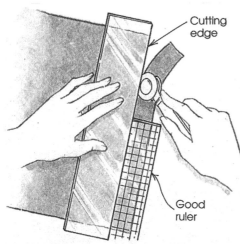

FIG. 23

Cutting edge

Good ruler

USING A CUTTING EDGE

I am a quilter who works template-free, so when I found a ruler that I thought was accurate, I didn't want to ruin it by using it as a cutting edge with a rotary cutter. Measuring along the straight grain of fabric, I use my good ruler to position my sturdy acrylic cutting edge, as shown in Fig. 23. When I am satisfied with the placement, I slide the good ruler out of the way and make my cut.

—Darcy Falk, Flagstaff, AZ

DON'T THROW OUT THAT CUTTING MAT

If you've got a cracked, warped, melted, or otherwise apparently ruined rotary cutting mat, don't throw it out without checking the size of any undamaged portions of the mat. A few snips with heavy kitchen shears and you'll have one or more small mats, ideal for taking to classes or using at your ironing board.

—Carwell Spiller, Colorado Springs, CO

AN INEXPENSIVE MAT FOR ROTARY CUTTERS

A relatively inexpensive cutting mat for rotary cutters is the vinyl mat designed to cover a drafting board. It's available at architecture and engineering supply stores and through mail-order catalogs. Board cover, as it's commonly called, is thin, heavy, and flexible, and self-healing when the surface is cut lightly. You can cut on either side of the mat. I've used my 38- by 60-in. mat for rotary cutting with great success for two years. If you were patient and careful, you could add gridlines to the mat with a fine permanent marker.

—Lori M. Graham, Muncie, IN

ROTARY CUTTER FOR PAPER

Buy an extra rotary cutter in a different color from your fabric one, or clearly label it "paper." Save old blades from fabric cutting in a child-proof container, and use them in the alternate cutter for cutting pattern paper or for other uses that might dull a new blade.

—Carol Stoner, Denver, CO

GREASE AS SOLVENT FOR LABEL GLUE

Even sewing tools are now plastered with those pesky price labels. When you try to peel the labels off, they leave a hard-to-remove sticky patch. While Bestine, a rubber-cement solvent, can remove the residue from some metals and glass, it is not recommended for use on plastic. Try rubbing a bit of grease, petroleum jelly, or shortening on the gummy area. Rub the glue and grease off with a paper towel.

—Betty Sager, Spring Valley, CA

REMOVING GLUE RESIDUE

The tip on removing glue residue from price labels on sewing tools caught my eye. Rubbing off glue with Skin-So-Soft bath oil from Avon is the best method that I've found, and much nicer than using petroleum jelly or shortening.

—*Florence Rand, Midland, TX*

HOMEMADE PATTERN WEIGHTS: THREE OPTIONS

A rotary cutter and mat can be a great time-saver for cutting out fabric, but I find commercial weights too small to hold pattern pieces properly. A parachutist friend of mine makes her own sewing weights out of nylon tubing.

Cut the tubing into the lengths you want. Sew one end closed, fill the tube with sand or buckshot, and sew the other end closed. The tubes are great because they will hold down the entire length of the pattern piece as you cut. A 1-ft. length filled with buckshot weighs about a pound.

—*Marcie Duston, Fitchburg, MA*

I make fabric weights out of metal bottle and jar lids in a variety of sizes (plastic caps will do). Remove the paper liner inside the cap and put a thin layer of modeling clay inside. Add a layer of BB shot, followed by another layer of clay, as shown in Fig. 24. Press down to fix the BBs in the clay. Add another layer of shot followed by clay to fill the cap. To seal the bottom, glue a piece of leather (try felt or Ultrasuede) to the last layer of clay. These weights store easily and won't break if dropped.

—*Mrs. Diana Wertz, Bremen, GA*

Here's how I make inexpensive dressmaker's weights: Put flat sinkers (available at sporting-goods stores) on a string and dip them in a jar of Plasticote, available at hardware stores. When they are dry, remove the string. The coating keeps your fingers away from the lead, and the weights (Fig. 25) are safe for use on all types of fabric. They stack three to four high and move easily in piles.

—*Tina Spiller, Colorado Springs, CO*

FIG. 24

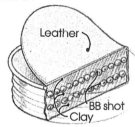

Leather

BB shot

Clay

FIG. 25

Chapter 3

❖

SEWING MACHINES
& SERGERS

WITHIN EASY REACH

My streamlined studio does not allow separate tables for my serger and sewing machine, so I placed both on a rotating particleboard platform, as shown in Fig. 26. To make the platform, first go to a local home center such as Home Depot and buy a 6-in. metal turntable unit that can support 300 lb. Figure the size board you'll need by placing both machines on a table back to back and measuring depth and length. Then mount the turntable on the center of the particleboard with the corners rounded off.

To lock the turntable in place so it doesn't spin, drill a hole through the board into the tabletop and insert a 3-in. bolt. Then remove the bolt and rotate the board until the other machine is in place. Now insert a marking pen up through the tabletop hole and mark a second hole on the board. Drill the second hole. You may have to unplug the front machine to rotate the platform.

—*Alis M. Wintle Sefick, Baldwinsville, NY*

FIG. 26

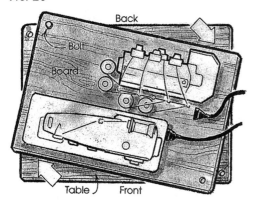

Back
Bolt
Board
Table
Front

THREAD TENSION

To check or adjust the thread tension of your sewing machine, thread the bobbin and top with different colors. When you sew your sample, it's easier to see if the tensions are correct.

—*Edith Frankel, Hannawa Falls, NY*

ADJUSTING BOBBIN TENSION

You can adjust the bobbin-case tension on most sewing machines, just as you can adjust the upper-thread tension, to ensure that the knot that forms between the upper and lower threads doesn't lie on the surface of the fabric. This adjustment may be necessary when working machine-embroidery stitches or stitching with unusual threads. On most machines, the bobbin tension is controlled by a tiny screw in the tension spring on the side of the bobbin case, as shown in Fig. 27. Before adjusting the bobbin tension, try adjusting the top-thread tension first; it's easier to do.

One of our colleagues offers the following rough but usable technique for setting and checking your bobbin tension. Insert a full bobbin in the case, with a few inches of thread ex-

FIG. 27

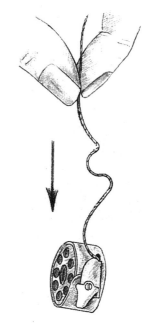

tending from the spring on the side. Holding the end of the thread, dangle the case like a yo-yo over your other hand. When the tension is correct, the case shouldn't slip down the thread unless you jerk lightly on the thread, and then it should slip about an inch each time. If it slips on its own, it's too loose; and if it doesn't slip at all, it's too tight. Adjust the tension by turning the screw on the spring counterclockwise a tiny amount to loosen, and clockwise to tighten. Usually, very small, less-than-quarter turns will be all that are required to correct the tension, but it's still a good idea to fiddle with that tiny screw only over a clean tabletop. If the screw drops on the floor, you may never see it again.

SPECIALTY MACHINE FEET

Three specialty feet available as accessories for most machines are the darning foot, the walking foot, and the roller foot (Fig. 28).

Use a darning foot for mending holes in garments or for free-motion embroidery. It attaches to the machine's needle bar so that when the needle is down, the foot holds the fabric and allows proper stitch formation; when the needle is up, the foot releases pressure on the fabric and you can move it in any direction. On most machines, you must lower the presser-foot release lever and the feed dog when using this foot.

For bulky or friction-inducing fabrics (like vinyl), or for multiple layers (like machine

quilting), the walking foot and the roller foot make life easier. A special toothed feeder on the walking foot moves in time with the feed dog to pull the top fabric layer forward. This keeps the layers from shifting. A roller foot achieves a similar end simply by rolling along over the top fabric layer and reducing drag on the foot.

END-OF-BOBBIN WARNING SIGNAL

After noticing that cash-register tapes change color as they near the end of the roll, I started marking the beginning of my bobbin thread as it winds onto the bobbin. I hold the tip of a washable marker against the thread as it winds until about a yard of thread from the end is marked. As soon as the color shows up as I stitch, I can stop and change the bobbin. This is a much more precise warning than the electronic signals some machines provide that always leave you guessing exactly how much thread you've got left after they start blinking.
—*Pat Sharp, Palo Alto, CA*

INVENTIVE STITCHING GUIDE

Put a rubber band around the free arm on your sewing machine to make a stitching guide for deep hems or curtain-rod pocket allowances. Since magnetic seam guides are not recom-

FIG. 28

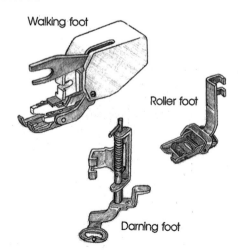

Walking foot

Roller foot

Darning foot

mended for electronic machines, a rubber band is ideal. It won't slip, doesn't mess up the machine, and costs nothing.
—*Nancy Camperud, Watsonville, CA*

QUILTING GUIDE

A quilting guide is a rod with a softly curved hook that helps in stitching widely spaced parallel lines, such as rows of machine embroidery. The adjustable guide attaches to the shank of the sewing machine, as shown in Fig. 29, and can be positioned either to the right or left of the post, providing a way to follow lines of stitching up to 3 or 4 in. away without marking the fabric. For greatest accuracy, keep your eyes on the guide and the previous stitching, not the new row, as you stitch.

FIG. 29

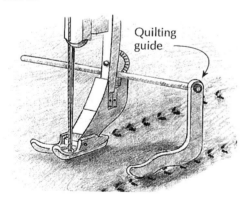

Quilting guide

FIG. 30A

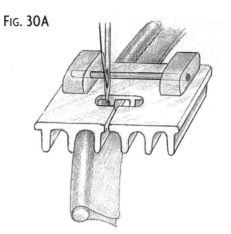

FIG. 30B

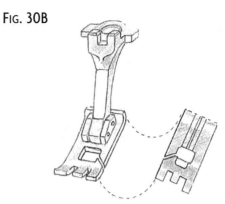

CORDING FOOT

A cording foot, also called a pin-tuck foot, has grooves on the bottom, which can help when stitching close to a strand of cord. To keep the stitching straight and in the correct position, lift the foot and position the bias-covered cord into one of the grooves; adjust the needle position (if possible) to stitch close to the cord. A foot such as the one shown in Fig. 30A, available from various sewing-machine companies, may have five to seven grooves on the bottom. The finer grooves are appropriate for smaller sizes of cord.

Many traditional buttonhole feet (Fig. 30B) have two grooves underneath and can also be used to stitch over fine cording. Again, adjust the needle position, if possible, to place the line of stitching close to the cord.

FIG. 31

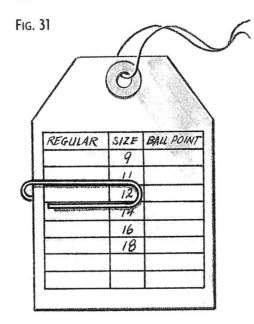

KEEPING TABS ON YOUR NEEDLE

A 2- by 3-in. manila hanging tag with a movable paper-clip marker (see Fig. 31) helps me keep track of which size or type of needle is in my sewing machine. I draw lines on the tag, but narrow-lined paper can be cut and glued onto the tag instead. The tag hangs easily from a spool spindle.

—*Gloria S. Fink, West Orange, NJ*

JEANS NEEDLE

Use a large-size jeans needle when sewing on many layers of dense fabrics. Its sharp point and thick shaft help to penetrate the fabric. The sharp needle is called the HJ by Schmetz and the Red Band by Singer. Choose the brand that is recommended for your model sewing machine.

WING NEEDLE

A wing needle has two metal extensions or wings, one on each side of the needle shaft. Used for machine embroidery and heirloom sewing, the wing needle creates decorative holes in the fabric during stitching.

This specialty needle is available as a single-wing needle or as a double-wing needle, which has one wing shaft and one regular needle shaft.

FIG. 32

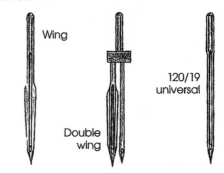

Wing needles (Fig. 32, left and center) work best on fabrics with a slightly loose weave. Use them with care: The wide extensions can damage fine fabrics and laces, causing distortion or breakage of fibers.

A size 120/19 universal needle is the largest size universal needle available (Fig. 32, right). The number before the slash indicates the width of the needle in millimeters (1.20mm), while the number after the slash follows the American needle sizing system, in which the needle gets larger as the number progresses from 8 to 19. A universal needle has a slightly rounded point that is appropriate for most fabrics. Try the extra-large 120/19 needle in place of a wing needle to create decorative holes in fine fabrics.

SPRING NEEDLE

A spring needle (Fig. 33) can be helpful when sewing free-motion machine embroidery with no presser foot and the feed dog dropped. When the needle moves down, the plastic extension at the lower end of the spring rests on the fabric and prevents flutter. When the needle moves up, the extension releases the fabric, leaving it free to move.

When the needle becomes dull or you need a different size, you don't have to replace the entire mechanism. Simply remove the needle by pressing down firmly on the top plastic collar

FIG. 33

(place the needle point into a cutting surface to avoid damaging it). Then insert a new sewing-machine needle, aligning the flat side of the needle with the flat portion of the collar opening. When you begin to sew, the spring will reseat itself on the needle shank.

SHIM

A spacer, or shim, works well to bridge a transition when sewing across a thick seam or varying layers of fabric. The tool, which can be fashioned from a piece of cardboard or purchased as a specialty sewing notion (such as the Jean-A-Ma-Jig or the Hump Jumper), helps to maintain the uniformity of machine stitching, especially on complex embroidery stitches. To use it, stitch until you reach the thicker area and the front of the presser foot begins to lift. With the needle in the fabric, raise the foot and place the spacer behind the foot, then lower the foot, as shown in Fig. 34. Leveling the foot allows the machine to continue stitching evenly.

SEWING-MACHINE PINCUSHION

When I sew, I often remove pins as I go. I used to end up with an annoying pile of pins that got in my way, fell on the floor, got lost in the machine's base, and generally drove me crazy—until I came up with this solution. I made a

FIG. 34

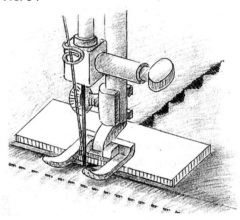

FIG. 35

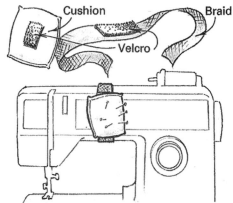

Sew Velcro onto a small, tightly stuffed cushion and a long braid strip. Pin it comfortably to sewing machine.

3- by 5-in. cushion from a scrap of material and stuffed it firmly with Polyfil. I sewed the fuzzy half of a piece of Velcro onto the back of the cushion and sewed the other side midway along a 15-in. length of ½-in.-wide braid. I wrapped the braid snugly around the body of my sewing machine, as shown in Fig. 35, and secured it with a safety pin. (You could also glue the Velcro to the front of the machine.) Now I have a pincushion in just the right place to receive the pins I take out in midseam. And it's removable for use at the cutting table or elsewhere.
—*Mary Applegate, Belchertown, MA*

ANOTHER PINCUSHION

Mary Applegate's sewing-machine pincushion is fine for people who own new sewing machines with a smooth body. But I suspect that there are many more sewers like me who own old machines that have a thread spindle or two sticking up from the top and all kinds of levers and controls on the front. On this kind of machine, there's no place to attach a pincushion.

The sewing circle I belong to makes a nifty alternative. We form a small cushion—about 1½ by 3 in.—from leftover fabric and stuff it with cornmeal or ground coffee. Either substance will give the pins just enough oil to prevent rusting. Then we attach the cushion to a narrow strap made of the same material, with a buttonhole or a slit in one end. The hole slips over the spool holder on top of the machine, and the cushion hangs either in front of or behind the body.
—*Phillida B. Mirk, Islesboro, ME*

NO-SLIP FOOT CONTROLS

I positioned my sewing-machine foot controls in a comfortable location on a piece of carpet remnant and marked closely around them with masking tape. Then I cut inside the masked pattern with a sharp utility knife. After cutting the holes and removing the tape, I put the carpet back under the sewing table with the foot controls in the cutouts.
—*Marie Van Bockern, Spokane, WA*

The foot control for my sewing machine used to creep, slide, and slither all the time—anything to get out of reach. I cut a piece of Jiffy Grip (used for feet in children's pajamas) to fit the foot and attached it with double-sided tape. I could have glued it, but tape makes it more removable and easier to replace. No more skids for me.
—*Iris Wilson, Victoria, British Columbia, Canada*

STAY-PUT FOOT PEDAL

To keep your sewing-machine foot pedal stationary when it rests on a carpet, apply the hook side of Velcro tape to the bottom of the pedal.
—*Gall Yano, Potomac, MD*

A KNEE-OPERATED FOOT PEDAL

I find a knee-operated control for my sewing machine much less fatiguing than the typical foot pedal that came with it, so I attached the pedal to my desk at knee height. I fastened two screw eyes to the right side of my sewing desk's knee opening, positioning them slightly farther apart than the width of the pedal. With the machine unplugged, I threaded wire through vent holes in the pedal case, pulling it taut against the case to avoid contact with any of the interior apparatus. Then I snugged the control to the desk with the screw eyes. It stays put without wiggling when I press it with my knee.

—Carol Stoner, Denver, CO

A DOUBLE-DUTY SURGE PROTECTOR

I like to keep my surge-protector strip and the cords plugged into it away from my feet, yet I need to unplug the strip to take with me and my machines to sewing workshops, where outlets are scarce. Gluing the rough side of hook and loop tape to the underside of my work table and the soft side of the tape to the surge-protector strip keeps the strip and cords out of my way, yet allows me to remove the protector easily.

—Deborah A. Martin, Indianapolis, IN

A BETTER SEWING-MAHINE BRUSH

Instead of cleaning my sewing machine with the brush that comes with it, I use a size 2 fan-shaped watercolor paint brush, available in any art-supply store for less than $2. The brush has a long handle, which enables me to reach out-of-the-way places easily. When used sideways, it will brush off larger areas, like the free arm, much faster than a standard brush will. My fan brush is also narrow enough to clean the tiny crevices in the bobbin case.

—Nancy Brockland, St. Louis, MO

HOW TO VACUUM SERGERS AND SEWING MACHINES

To clean my serger and sewing machine, I attach a flexible drinking straw to the crevice attachment of my regular vacuum cleaner, closing the space between the straw and the crevice tool with masking tape. This works so well that I bought an extra crevice tool just so I could have one ready to go all the time.

—Elizabeth Rymer, Hurricane Mills, TN

A CLEANER SEWING MACHINE WITH PIPE CLEANERS

Fluffy pipe cleaners are ideal tools to use to clean out your bobbin case area. Pipe cleaners can be bent into various shapes to get into corners, to go around bends, and to remove dust, thread, and lint.

—*Clary Hannan, Watkins Glen, NY*

SAFE PLASTIC CLEANER

Red-dyed fabrics tend to leave a red residue on the bed and plastic parts of my sewing machine. This unsightly film is difficult to remove and often stains other fabrics. I take it off with a non-acetone nail-polish remover that contains ethyl acetate and alcohol. Don't use one with acetone, which will damage the plastic parts on your machine.

—*Jean Kaplan, Phoenix, AZ*

TOWARD A TIDY SEWING ROOM

To prevent mess in my sewing room, I tape a 9- by 12-in. plastic bag to my table on the right-hand side of the machine for clipped threads and trimmings. Here's how to keep the bag open: Cut a ¼-in. circular strip from around a plastic bleach bottle. To make it fit the bag opening, cut the circle apart, fit it inside the plastic bag, ends overlapping, fold the bag over it twice, and staple around the bag right through the plastic. Tape or staple the open bag where it will be a convenient mess-catcher. You can sew a fabric bag for a coordinated sewing room.

My serger doesn't have a catch bin, so I improvise. I used a 6½-in.-diameter metal ring from my macramé things and another 9- by 12-in. plastic bag. The ring slips inside the plastic bag very snugly. If yours doesn't, use a larger bag and staple around the ring after folding the bag over it. Slip the ring under the serger at the spot where the trimmings fall.

—*Shirley Hastings, Kamloops, British Columbia, Canada*

THREAD SCRAPS

I have a carpeted sewing room and dislike having to vacuum snippets of thread from the rug every time I sew. Recently, I started using this old technique of my mother's. Place a small container with about ½ in. of water in it beside the sewing machine; an empty margarine tub is just right. Whenever you clip a thread, remove basting, or unpick, just drop the bits of thread into the water. Even if there is a breeze, the thread pieces stay put. I also place a little water in the thread catcher of my serger, which reduces daily vacuuming drastically.

—*Caroline Wallace, Barstow, CA*

SPOOL WINDER

We recently purchased a three-thread serger and suddenly needed three threads of the same color for a project. We found that a standard electric hand mixer with only one of its blades inserted made an excellent spool winder, as shown in Fig. 36. Wrap the thread around the spool to start it. You can wind the thread at three speeds, and since the blades rotate toward the center, this method works whether you're right-handed or left-handed, depending on which blade you use. If your cone is too narrow

FIG. 36

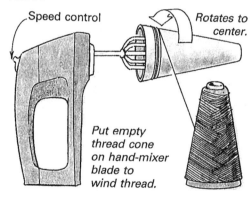

Speed control

Rotates to center.

Put empty thread cone on hand-mixer blade to wind thread.

for the blade, you can tape a cardboard extension inside the small cone, or you can snug it onto a larger cone for winding. Use the other blade to unwind if necessary.

—*Eve and Amy Eagan, Wyncote, PA*

BOBBIN SPOOL WINDER

I like to have matching thread on my serger but hate to buy four cones of one color, each with 5,000 m. per cone. I use a handy bob (for keeping matching bobbin and thread together) to fill empty, regular-size thread spools.

First I snip off the little thread holders around the outer edge of the handy bob so they won't catch on the machine. Then I put a bobbin on the sewing machine, as if to fill it. I put the handy bob on the bobbin (double-faced tape makes it adhere well) and place the empty spool on the handy bob with the thread groove on top (Fig. 37). The bobbin turns the handy bob, which turns the spool, and I guide the thread by hand to fill the spool evenly. This way, one cone fills as many spools as I need.

—*Shirley Hastings, Kamloops, British Columbia, Canada*

CHANGING SERGER NEEDLES

Changing a serger overlock needle, especially the round type, can be a real chore. If the eye doesn't point directly at the operator, the machine won't sew correctly. Here's a simple solution. Make sure the scarf (the indented side of the needle) faces the rear. Insert the needle into the holder, and hold it up in the proper position by putting a pin point through its eye. Then tighten the screw.

—*Mary Jane McClelland, Diamond Bar, CA*

FIG. 37

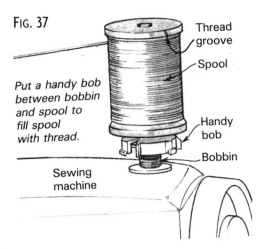

Thread groove

Spool

Put a handy bob between bobbin and spool to fill spool with thread.

Handy bob

Bobbin

Sewing machine

THREE TIPS FOR THREADING A SERGER

It's a lot easier to slip threads through all the tricky loops and holes when you're threading your serger if you stiffen the thread ends with Fray Check first. Put a drop between your thumb and forefinger and draw the last 3 in. or so of thread through the drop. Drying takes only a moment.

—*Erin Nesmith, Enid, OK*

I used to have trouble threading my serger with soft thread, but not any more. I spray a little hairspray on a piece of paper, pick some up on my fingers, and apply it to the end of the thread. I let it dry, clip the thread end, and presto—I have a perfect needle threader. Don't try to spray the thread; always use your fingers.

—*Effie Johnson, Sapulpa, OK*

For hassle-free serger threading, cut the old color threads close to the cones, place the new color on the thread stand, and tie the new color on with an overhand knot. Then serge slowly until the new color comes through. On my machine, only the needle must be rethreaded, so when the knot gets close to the needle eye, I clip out the knot and slip the new color through the eye.

—*Susan Riley, Sudbury, MA*

SERGER TAILS

You can use your loop-turner tool, a long piece of stiff wire with a latch on one end, to avoid cutting the tail off a serged seam and leaving a frayed edge. Run the latch of the loop turner under the loops on the underside for about 2 in. until you reach the edge. Catch the tail with the latch, and making sure it closes, pull the tail through the loops.

—*Rita Jacobson, Fountain Valley, CA*

INSERTING A NEW SERGER NEEDLE

To put in a new needle more easily, thread the needle before you insert it. Then, holding the thread taut in one hand and guiding the needle with the other, insert the needle into the needle bar. The tension on the thread will hold the needle in place while you tighten the screw, and if you drop the needle it won't get lost.

—*F. Novarra, Tualatin, OR*

PREMARK TENSION ON KNOBS

Do you have to return your serger tension knobs to zero each time you rethread your machine? If so, mark the recommended tension settings required for standard size thread on each knob

with red nail polish. After you thread your serger, you can quickly return the knobs to their original tension settings by aligning the machine guides with your red marks. You'll also have quick reference points if you have to adjust the tensions up or down to accommodate a special technique, such as a rolled hem, or nonstandard thread weights.
—*Susan Strange, Glencoe, IL*

DIFFERENTIAL FEED

Many of the newer sergers have adjustable, or differential, feed mechanisms, which means that the feed dogs have been divided into two sets, one in front of the needle and one behind it. By adjusting the differential feed control, you can choose to have the two sets move at the same speed, or to have one set move faster than the other. A setting of 1, or normal, means that the fabric you're serging will move under the foot at the same rate that it moves out at the back, as on sergers without differential feed. Settings below 1 mean that the rear set will move fabric away from the needle faster than the front set moves it in, which stretches the fabric slightly as it gets stitched. This is useful in preventing puckering on some sheers, or for making lettuce edges on stretchy fabrics.

Settings above 1 cause the front set to move fabric into the needle faster than the rear set moves it away, which eases or compresses the fabric as it gets stitched. This is ideal for stretchy fabrics that tend to ripple when they are stitched.

MAGNETIZED SCREWDRIVERS

I keep my serger screwdrivers on a magnetic pin holder, such as a Grabbit, which magnetizes them. This makes it easier for me to maneuver those tiny screws when I'm changing needles, feet, etc. It's especially helpful for anyone with arthritis. You can use this technique for sewing-machine screwdrivers too, but if your machine is electronic be careful because it could be sensitive to magnets.
—*Barbara Worden, Mechanicsburg, PA*

Chapter 4

CONSTRUCTION TECHNIQUES

STAYSTITCHING

Staystitching is applied along seamlines before assembling a garment to prevent stretching and distortion of the seamlines. This step is essential on a stretchy fabric such as one that is finely pleated or on bias edges. On a single layer of fabric, stitch just inside the seamline in the seam allowance, as shown in Fig. 38. Use a short to medium stitch length, and avoid stretching the seamline while staystitching.

FIG. 38

BIAS

A garment section cut on the bias, so that the bias of the fabric hangs vertically, is flexible and molds itself to the body more than if it was cut on the straight grain. All bias cuts are not the same. True bias intersects the lengthwise and crosswise grains of woven fabric at 45°. Partial bias intersects them at any other angle (except 90°), and has less stretch than true bias. To find the true bias, straighten a crossgrain edge (by tearing or pulling a thread) and fold it up to the selvage as shown in Fig. 39. The resulting diagonal fold is on the true bias.

Most garment sections have some edges that are on the bias. For example, the shoulder seam of a bodice and the side seam of an A-line skirt usually lie on the partial bias. A bias-cut edge of fabric can easily stretch during machine stitching, so avoid pulling the fabric as you stitch, or use an even-feed foot. When you wear a garment with bias areas, gravity may cause stretching and result in an uneven hem. To reduce this problem, hang garments for several days before you hem them.

SEWING DARTS

My friend Peter has a fabulous method of sewing darts that's perfect for sheer fabric or just a clean look. He pulls up the bobbin thread (a foot or so for an average dart); then, with the

FIG. 39

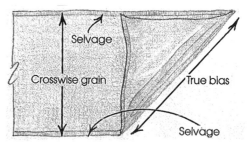

FIG. 40

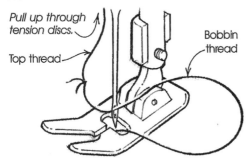

Pull up through tension discs.

Top thread

Bobbin thread

FIG. 41

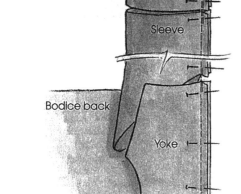

Cuff

Cuff

Sleeve

Bodice back

Yoke

bobbin thread, he threads the needle from the side opposite the groove. He ties the bobbin thread to the top thread and, retracing the path of the top thread, as shown in Fig. 40, pulls the bobbin thread up through the tension guides, removing the slack. This way the machine sews with only one thread, so when he starts sewing the dart at the tip there are no loose ends.

—*M. Elaine MacKay, Thamesford, Ontario, Canada*

BATCHING SEAMS SAVES TIME

Here's a manufacturing technique that can save you time in garment construction: Sew all the seams you can at the same time with a continuous line of stitching. Pin or baste any seam that doesn't intersect another and arrange the seams in your lap one on top of the other so you can reach for them quickly. Sew your first seam; backstitch at the beginning and end. There won't be any thread tails to tie off, because you are going to butt the next seam up against the first (see Fig. 41). Continue sewing all of the seams you have prepared. When all the seams are sewn, cut them apart and press the seam allowances open. Repeat the process till the garment is sewn.

—*Catherine Neff, Muscoda, WI*

CLIPPING SEAM ALLOWANCES

Clip or notch curved seam allowances to relieve stress and remove excess fabric so they'll lie flat after pressing. It's easy to forget when to clip (snip from the fabric edge just to the stitching line) and when to notch (cut wedges of fabric out of the seam allowances). Look at the outer edge of the seam allowance after stitching but before pressing or turning. If the edge is shaped like a *c*, as in a faced neckline (see Fig. 42), you'll need to *clip* the seam allowance to allow it to spread when the garment is turned right side out and keep the facing from rolling outward. If the edge is shaped like an *n*, as in a round collar, it must be *notched* to remove excess fabric so that the collar will press flat with no lumps.

FIG. 42

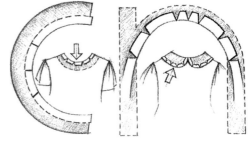

FIG. 43

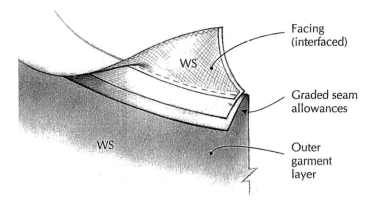

Facing
(interfaced)

Graded seam
allowances

Outer
garment
layer

GRADING SEAM ALLOWANCES

Seam allowances may need to be graded, or trimmed, to reduce bulk and/or prevent the formation of a ridge that shows through on the right side of the garment. Grading involves trimming the width of the layers in graduated fashion, with the allowance closest to the outermost garment layer the widest and the bottom layer the narrowest. Seam allowances that are enclosed (as in a neck-edge seam) and multiple layers of bulky fabrics usually require grading.

Before grading, press the seam allowances thoroughly. Trim the seam allowance farthest from the outer garment layer first, to ¼ in. Trim each subsequent seam allowance ⅛ in. wider, as shown in Fig. 43. Trim the sewn-in interfacing as close to the seam as possible. Fabrics that ravel easily may need slightly wider seam allowances to maintain the integrity of the seamline.

EDGE STITCHING

You can use edge stitching to complete a seam from the right side. For example, in bagging a lining, you can't finish the slit in the sleeve underarm seam by stitching with right sides together. So, after turning the sleeve inside out, push the seam allowances of the lining's open section to the inside. Pull gently at the ends of the opening to align the folds, pin them together, and topstitch through all four layers as close to the fold as possible, as shown in Fig. 44.

FINISHING SEAMS

Clean finish the raw edges of your garment pieces either before assembly or after stitching the seams to prevent them from fraying. Among the most common methods are: turning under ¼ in. and straight stitching close to the folded

FIG. 44

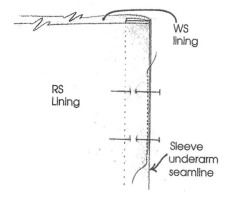

WS
lining

RS
Lining

Sleeve
underarm
seamline

FIG. 45A

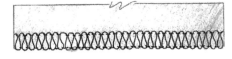

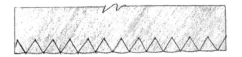

FIG. 45B

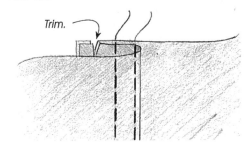

Trim.

edge (Fig. 45A, at bottom); machine zigzagging close to the raw edge (middle); and overcasting the raw edge using a serger or domestic sewing machine with an overcast stitch (top).

For a clean-finished, ready-to-wear look, try finishing seams with a double row of topstitching. You can use a seam such as the mock flat-felled seam, also called a double-welt seam, as shown in Fig. 45B. With the fabric right sides together, sew a normal ⅝-in. seam, then press the seam allowances to one side and topstitch twice from the right side, once close to the seamline and again ¼ in. away. To reduce raveling, trim seam allowances to ⅜ in. For bulky fabrics, you can trim the seam allowance next to the garment to ¼ in. before topstitching.

STITCHING SEAMS OPEN

To keep seam allowances pressed open in places such as crotch curves, first sew the seam and press the allowances together. Fold and press one seam allowance back, lapping it over the seamline onto the other seam allowance by ¹⁄₁₆ in., as shown in Fig. 46. Stitch through both seam allowances on the edge of the fold. Then turn the garment right side out and press the seam open. In deep curves such as the crotch, trim the seam allowances to ¼ in.
—*Elaine Rutledge, Chunchula, AL*

FIG. 46

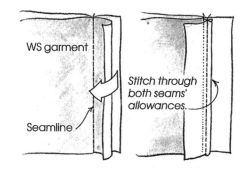

WS garment

Seamline

Stitch through both seams' allowances.

FRENCH SEAM

A French seam encloses the raw edge of a seam allowance and requires two passes of straight stitches. It's effective on transparent fabrics where a raw edge would be visible, and for fabrics that ravel. French seams work best on straight to slightly curved seams. First stitch with wrong sides together, at half the seam allowance width for medium-weight fabrics, as shown in Fig. 47. (For thicker fabrics, stitch closer to the raw edge to allow for the fabric taken up in the fold, or turn, of the cloth.) Press seam open, then fold right sides together and press again. Trim raw edges if necessary, so they fall within the seamline. Stitch, right sides together, on the seamline.

FIG. 47

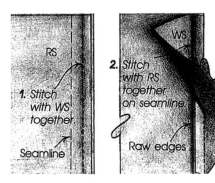

VISUAL AID FOR FRENCH SEAMS

It's a lot easier to see the first seam of a French seam that you're trying to trim, before turning it, if you sew it in a contrasting thread. You'll be able to trim closer without worrying about catching a thread.

—Janet McGlynn, Neenah, WI

EXTRA PRESSING MAKES A BETTER FRENCH SEAM

After the first step in a French seam (making a narrow seam with wrong sides together), I always take the time to press the seam open flat after trimming. Then I fold the seam over right sides together and press again. The first pressing is an extra step, but it helps roll that first line of stitching to the exact outer edge.

—Deborah C. Little, Alva, FL

REDUCING SHOW-THROUGH

To reduce seam allowance show-through on lightweight, lacy, or sheer fabrics, you can finish the seam allowances in a false French seam. After sewing a normal ⅝-in. seam right sides together, press the seam flat, then press it open; fold each seam allowance in half toward the center, and edgestitch together close to the fold, as shown in Fig. 48.

FLAT-FELL SEAM

A flat-fell seam is an attractive, double-stitched method of enclosing both raw edges of a straight or slightly curved seam, such as the armscye of a dropped shoulder shirt. With wrong sides together, sew a regular ⅝-in. seam. Press the seam allowances open, then to one side (you can place the fell to either side, but be sure to match corresponding seams in a garment). Trim the in-

FIG. 48

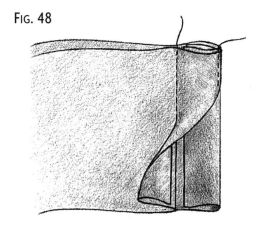

FIG. 49

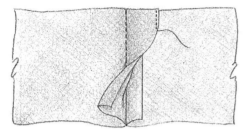

ner seam allowance to ⅛ in., and press the edge of the outer (top) seam allowance under ¼ in.

Stitch this folded edge down as shown in Fig. 49. Be sure that your folded width remains uniform, with the stitching straight and close to the fold, since the seam will show from the right side.

ALTERNATIVE FLAT-FELL SEAM

Here's a quick alternative to basting and pressing a flat-fell sleeve seam. Trim the sleeve seam allowance to ⅜ in., and press it toward the right side of the sleeve. Now slip the armscye seam allowance, also trimmed to ⅜ in., into the fold so the raw edge just butts up to the crease. Stitch through all three thicknesses in a ¼-in. seam. Press the seam fiat and topstitch on the right side.

HONG KONG SEAM

A Hong Kong seam finish, which binds the edges of seam allowances with a non-raveling bias strip of fabric, is ideal for finishing the inside of an unlined garment, such as a gabardine coat. The binding keeps the fabric from raveling, and should be lightweight lining fabric so it won't stiffen the seam. A Hong Kong binding is usually added after a seam is sewn and before any crossing seams are stitched.

Press seam allowances open. Align the edges of bias strip and seam allowance and stitch ⅛ in. from the edge, as shown at left in Fig. 50. Press the bias around the edge to cover the stitching (right). Stitch in the ditch of the seam through the seam allowance and unfolded bias.

FIG. 50

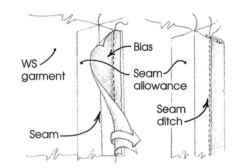

WS garment

Bias

Seam allowance

Seam

Seam ditch

SECURING FUSIBLE INTERFACING

I often use fusible non-woven interfacing for yokes, collars, and cuffs. Since non-woven interfacings tend to fuzz after repeated washings, I use them only in enclosed areas. Fusible interfacing can also come loose, even after careful fusing; so here's how I prevent that. I place a sheet of tracing paper under the interfacing and use my tracing wheel to trace the seamline. Then I cut the interfacing with pinking shears just outside the seamline. I fuse and sew as usual. The stitching just catches the pinked edges.
—*Patricia Clements, Madison, TN*

BOUND EDGE

Sewing a narrow bound edge makes a beautiful finishing detail for fine garments such as lingerie. First, cut 1-in. bias strips from the garment fabric. You can use a ¼-in.-wide No. 3 bias-tape maker to fashion the required ¼-in.-wide double-fold tape.

Bias binding is applied with no stretching or ease. Open the bias strip and match the cut edges of the bias and garment with right sides together. Machine- or hand-stitch the strip in place along the fold line. Do not trim the seam. Fold the bias over and around the raw edge and slip-stitch the binding to the inside of the garment, as shown in Fig. 51.

LINING EASE

When you fully line a garment, it's a good idea to add ease to the inner layer by cutting the lining larger than the fashion fabric. The extra lining ease allows the lining to absorb the strain of sitting, stretching, and arm movement without pulling on and distorting the outer fabric or the smooth drape of the garment.

The easiest way to add ease in the width is to make a center-back pleat in the lining, usually about 1 in. deep (see Fig. 52), which adds 2 in. of ease to the lining. To add ease to the length of the lining, cut the lining 1 in. longer than the body of the garment and ¼ in. longer than the finished sleeve length to allow the lining hem to blouse over the garment hem.

FIG. 52

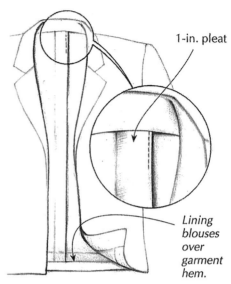

1-in. pleat

Lining blouses over garment hem.

FIG. 51

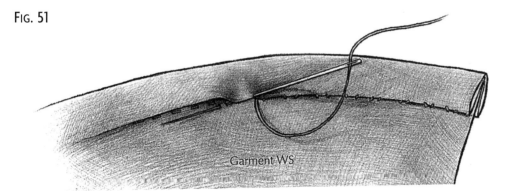

Garment WS

FIG. 53

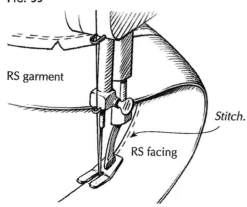

RS garment

RS facing

Stitch.

UNDERSTITCHING

Understitching keeps facings from rolling to the outside and gives a crisp edge to the garment. To prepare for understitching, grade and clip the seam allowances with the garment's allowance wider than the facing's, then press allowances to lie smoothly under the facing. On the facing, straight-stitch close to the seamline through all thicknesses, as shown in Fig. 53.

SEWING SHARP POINTS

To make sharp points, sew regulation stitches until you're 1 in. from the corner. Then make very small stitches to the point. Sew two or three tiny stitches across the point, depending on the thickness of the fabric. Next, trim close to the small stitches and cut across the point (Fig. 54A). Turn the fabric right side out and insert a needle that's threaded with doubled, unknotted thread on each side of the point through the seam (Fig. 54B). Pull gently on the thread to sharpen the point.

—*Ilya Sandra Perlingieri, San Diego, CA*

REINFORCED CORNERS LOOK CRISPER

Are you having trouble sewing sharp corner angles à la Miyake, or kimono gusset sleeves? Here's a trick that will help to make those inset

FIG. 54A

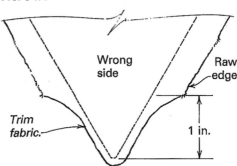

Wrong side

Raw edge

Trim fabric.

1 in.

FIG. 54B

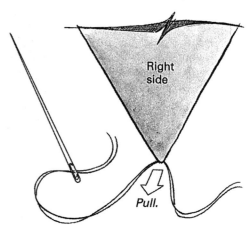

Right side

Pull.

corners neater and stronger: Reinforce the corners of the angle with a piece of lining or self fabric if the fabric is lightweight. After marking the seamlines, cut a piece of lining 2½ in. square and place the center of the square over the marked corner on the right side of the garment, aligning the grainline with the stitching line (see step 1 in Fig. 55). Sew the two fabrics together with short stitches following the seamline just into the seam allowance. Staystitch the entire seam if the pattern calls for it. To complete the process, see steps 2-4. When stitching the garment together, stitch just next to the reinforcing stitches on the seamline, and make sure that the reinforcing fabric is pulled flat.

—*Jeltje Matthys, Port Hope, Ontario, Canada*

FIG. 55

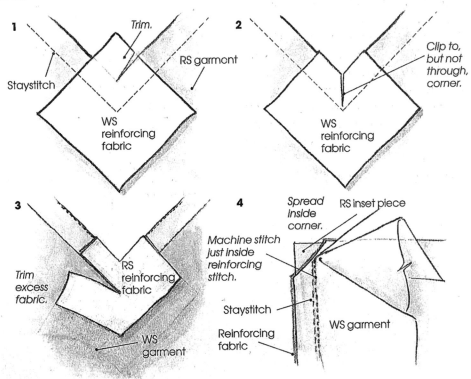

FIG. 56

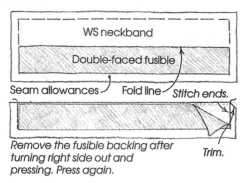

WS neckband

Double-faced fusible

Seam allowances — Fold line — *Stitch ends.*

Remove the fusible backing after turning right side out and pressing. Press again.   Trim.

SEWING CRISP KNIT NECKBANDS

I have a neat way to make professional-looking knit neckbands. Cut the collar or neckband pattern as usual out of commercial knit ribbing. Cut a piece of Wonder Under or other double-faced fusible half the width of the neckband, without seam allowances. Press the fusible to one-half of the neckband on the wrong side (see Fig. 56). Using the paper backing as a stitching guide, sew the neckband ends right sides together. Trim the seams and corners, then turn and press. Remove the paper backing and press again, fusing the front to the back. Stitch the completed neckband into the garment as your pattern instructions direct.

—*Cindy Peterson, Myrtle Point, OR*

SLEEVES FOR REVERSIBLE GARMENTS

Raglan, dolman, and kimono sleeves (Fig. 57) all are good choices for reversible garments, because their flat construction rarely involves easing. While the shapes of these sleeves can vary widely, the basic structure of each is simple. The seams of raglan sleeves extend diagonally from the underarm to the neckline. Dolman sleeves have no armscye seams; they're cut in one with the garment front and back. Kimono sleeves, set in at a right angle to the garment, are usually wide, simple tubes, like the sleeves on the tradi-

tional Japanese garment they're named for. Kimono sleeves can also be cut in one with the garment shoulder, like dolman sleeves.

FIG. 57

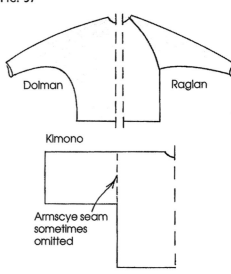

Dolman   Raglan

Kimono

Armscye seam sometimes omitted

SETTING IN SLEEVES

My method of setting a sleeve was born of my distaste for the "easy" cuff-to-hem method. It creates a continuous armhole seam with no underarm distortion. I also use it for pants and three-piece sleeves—especially those that do not have seams to match in the jacket body. It works equally well with French seams.

Sew the shoulder seam and press it open. Sew two rows of long stitches for easing between the notches on the sleeve cap. Then stitch the sleeve to the bodice, leaving about 1½ in. from the side seams unstitched, as at top center in Fig. 58. Fold the right sides of the sleeve together and the right sides of the bodice together. Sew the sleeve and bodice underarm seams separately and press them open, as shown at bottom center in the drawing. Finally, match the underarm seam and stitch.

—Eleanor L. Shields, Santa Rosa, CA

SET-IN SLEEVES

Staystitch the entire sleeve cap. Then clip the bobbin thread at the front and back notches and pull up the ease. Sew with the sleeve on top, right sides together. To manipulate the ease so the cap will be perfectly rounded with no tucks or puckers, I use the tip of a pencil eraser to ease in the fullness on the seam-allowance side of the needle close to the staystitching as I machine-stitch.

—Dorothy Richards, Escondido, CA

SET-IN SLEEVES WITHOUT EASE BASTING

Set-in sleeves with a moderate amount of ease in the cap can be smoothly set to the armscye without ease basting. Match and pin the underarm seams, the notches, the small dots, and the top of the cap to the shoulder seam. Place the

FIG. 58

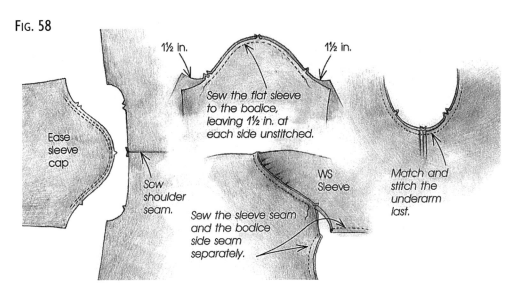

Ease sleeve cap

Sew shoulder seam.

Sew the flat sleeve to the bodice, leaving 1½ in. at each side unstitched.

1½ in.   1½ in.

WS Sleeve

Sew the sleeve seam and the bodice side seam separately.

Match and stitch the underarm last.

bodice piece uppermost and the sleeve against the feed dogs; begin stitching at the underarm.

When you get to the first notch, you must begin to allow for ease in the sleeve piece by placing your left hand between the two garment pieces and working the ease evenly into the area between the notch and the first small dot pin with your fingertips. Anchor the ease by pulling gently with your right hand on the upper-bodice fabric from the next pin; this maneuver will flatten and control the ease you have just introduced. Maintain a gentle pressure on the bodice piece as you sew each section of the seam. You will be surprised at how much ease you can incorporate, and you won't get those unsightly

FIG. 59

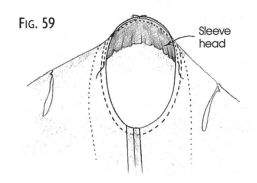

Sleeve head

puckers in the bodice that occur when a sleeve is inadvertently gathered too much for the size of the armscye.

—*Stephanie Tretick, Pittsburgh, PA*

SLEEVE HEAD

To give body and support to the sleeve cap of a jacket or blouse, you sometimes need a sleeve head (Fig. 59). This is a bias strip of fabric about 7½ in. by 2¼ in. which is sewn inside the sleeve cap after the sleeve has been sewn to the garment. The stitching line is in the sleeve seam allowance, but very close to the sleeve stitching. The material used varies from lambswool in jackets to self fabric in blouses.

FIG. 60

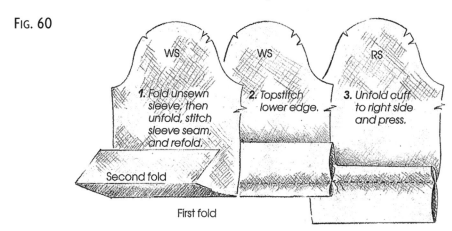

WS

1. Fold unsewn sleeve; then unfold, stitch sleeve seam, and refold.

Second fold

First fold

WS

2. Topstitch lower edge.

RS

3. Unfold cuff to right side and press.

ONE-PIECE SLEEVE AND CUFF

This one-piece sleeve and cuff works best for short sleeves. It can also work with long sleeves, but because the cuff doesn't unbutton, it needs to be wider than the hand. The finished cuff will have the same directional pattern as the sleeve.

Add twice the desired width of the cuff plus ¾ in. to the length of the finished sleeve. Before sewing the sleeve seam, measure the cuff's width from the bottom of the fabric's WS, and press a fold. Press another fold where the raw edge meets the inside fold of the fabric, as shown in Fig. 60. Unfold the material and sew the sleeve seam, matching the fold lines. With the sleeve WS out, refold following the pressed fold lines, then topstitch ¼ to ⅜ in. from the lower folded edge through all layers. Finally, with RS out, unfold the cuff downward as shown, and press.

—*Mary Hardenbrook, Huntington Beach, CA*

PREVENTING SHOULDER-PAD SHOW-THROUGH

Shoulder pads can be real eyesores if their outlines show through light-colored clothing. I cover mine with flesh-colored lining matched to my skin tone, and the outlines disappear. Cut a square with a bias length slightly longer than

FIG. 61

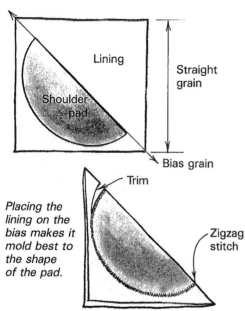

Placing the lining on the bias makes it mold best to the shape of the pad.

the outer edge of the pad, as shown in Fig. 61. Lay the pad on the cloth with the long edge on the bias, and fold the cloth over the pad. Pin it in place, zigzag or overcast along the curved edge of the pad, and trim off the excess fabric.

—*Elisheva Bush, Jerusalem, Israel*

REFINING A DROPPED SHOULDER

Patterns for dropped- or extended-shoulder garments have straight shoulder seams, but similar ready-to-wear garments have rounded ones. You can refine your pattern by taking off ½ in. from the armscye on both the bodice back and front at the shoulder line, as shown in step 1 of Fig. 62. Take 1 in. out of the sleeve pattern with a ½-in.-deep tuck along the shoulder line, as shown in step 2. The sleeve cap for this type of sleeve should have little, if any, ease. If the pattern you are using includes ease, remove it at the underarm after stitching the sleeve to the bodice (steps 3 and 4) and checking the right side of the garment for appearance.

—*Margaret Komives, Milwaukee, WI*

FIG. 62

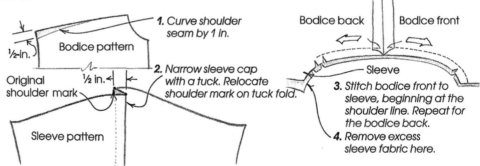

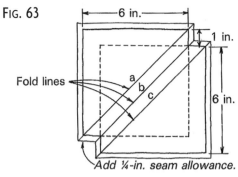

FIG. 63

6 in.

1 in.

6 in.

Fold lines

a
b
c

Add ¼-in. seam allowance.

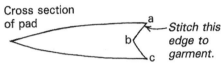

Cross section
of pad

a
b
c

← Stitch this
edge to
garment.

PLEATED SHOULDER PADS

Here is a shoulder-pad pattern with a pleat built into the armhole edge. The pleat allows you to machine-sew this edge to the garment seam allowance without flattening the pad.

Draw a 6-in. square. Then draw another 6-in. square, offset by 1 in., as shown in Fig. 63. Draw the fold lines a, b, and c. Add a ¼-in. seam allowance around the outline of the two squares. This pattern makes one complete pad cover, so cut out two at a time.

—*Pat Norman, Modesto, CA*

SHOULDER-PAD POCKETS FOR REVERSIBLE JACKETS

Reversible jackets are inspiring but don't easily allow shoulder pads. Creating a shoulder-yoke pocket with a button closure to hold the pads solves the problem and adds a nice design detail. Cut a yoke pocket in one piece that fits the shoulder of your jacket with enough ease to hold the shoulder pad you are using. You can easily make a pattern by joining the front and back jacket pattern pieces to create one. Top-stitch the back edge of the pocket to the jacket

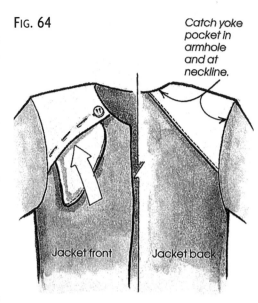

FIG. 64

Catch yoke
pocket in
armhole
and at
neckline.

Jacket front   Jacket back

back (see Fig. 64). Sew buttonholes to the yoke-pocket edge and flat, shankless buttons to the jacket. When you reverse the jacket, switch the shoulder pads.

—*Melissa Ennis, Arlington, VA*

READY-TO-WEAR TECHNIQUE FOR SKIRTS

Here's a slick method for attaching the lining and waistband all at once to a skirt. It's taken directly from a designer garment I worked on in my alteration business. Prepare each piece separately: skirt (seams sewn, zipper installed), lining (seams sewn, pleats formed or ease-stitched at waist and the opening for the zipper pressed back), and waistband (interfaced and very carefully marked with notches, etc.). Sew one long edge of the waistband to the skirt, right sides together, easing in the skirt as usual. Then press the seam toward the waistband. Sew the other long edge of the waistband to the lining, right sides together, and press this seam toward the lining. Fold the waistband along the fold line, wrong sides together, at the same time inserting the lining inside the skirt (see Fig. 65). Press the fold line, making sure that the lining/waistband seam is ⅛ in. higher than, rather than aligned with, the skirt/waistband seam, as shown in the drawing. Now fold the waistband on the fold line so that right sides are together (you can probably do this without having to pull out the lining), and sew just the short ends of the waistband. Turn the band right side out and press. To finish the lower edge of the under-lap, clip the waistband seam allowance as shown where the lining ends and the underlap begins. Stitch in the ditch from the right side to finish the rest of the waistband, then slip-stitch the underlap and finish the rest of the skirt as you would any other lined skirt.

—Samina Mirza, Katy, TX

FIG. 65

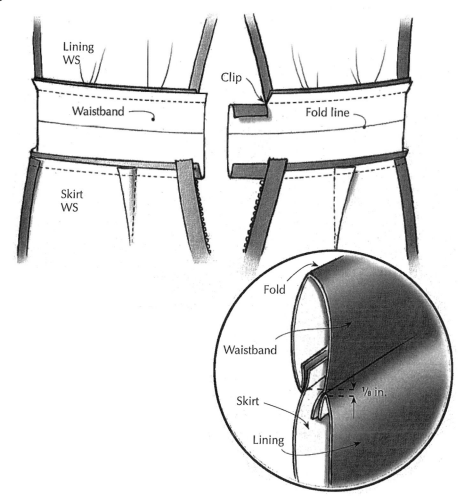

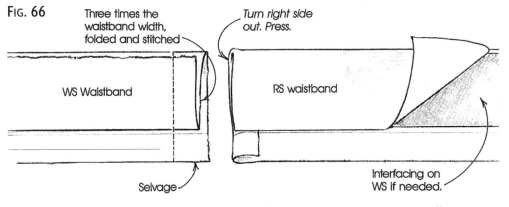

FIG. 66

Three times the waistband width, folded and stitched

Turn right side out. Press.

WS Waistband

RS waistband

Selvage

Interfacing on WS if needed.

SELF-INTERFACED WAISTBAND

For a neat, easy waistband, I cut a strip from the selvage edge of my fabric three times the width of the finished band, plus the selvage itself, and 5 in. longer than the waist measurement (for overlap and seam allowances). Then, with the right side facing me, and the selvage on the bottom, I fold the band in thirds (see Fig. 66), leaving the selvage free. I stitch across the ends, turn the waistband right side out, and press. If the fabric is very soft, I may add fusible interfacing to the wrong side next to the selvage.

To sew the band to the waistline in one step, I pin it in place with the fold on the outside and the selvage extending over the seamline on the inside. I stitch it by machine from the outside, sewing very close to the fold and catching the selvage on the inside.

—*Jeanette Bernstein, Cranston, RI*

STITCHING IN THE DITCH

Here's a fast way to finish the inside of a waistband, collar, or cuff, without hand-stitching. After stitching the seam, turn under the raw edge and pin it ⅛ in. below the seamline (see Fig. 67). Machine-sew on the right side of the fabric, in the "ditch" of the seam. While stitching, pull the fabric apart gently, on either side of the seam. The machine stitching will be virtually invisible on the right side of the garment, and the inside will have a clean, finished look.

—*Janaford Jones, Altadena, CA*

FIG. 67

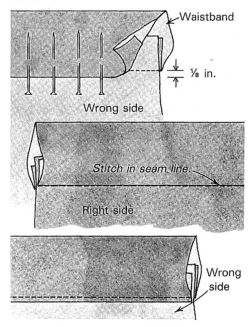

Waistband

⅛ in.

Wrong side

Stitch in seam line.

Right side

Wrong side

WAISTBAND CLOSURES

You can comfortably custom-fit a waistband with hooks and eyes or bar fasteners. But to ensure stability and keep the short waistband extension from showing, sew another hook and eye or fastener near the top corner of the extension, in the opposite direction of the other fasteners (Fig. 68). The second hook-and-eye provides a stable counterpull.

—Shirley Kates, Newtown, CT

FIG. 68

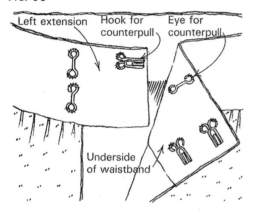

Left extension | Hook for counterpull | Eye for counterpull

Underside of waistband

EASY ELASTIC FOR WAISTBANDS

In making pants or skirts with the waistband cut in one with the garment, I found threading elastic through the waistband difficult because it caught under the loose edges of the seam allowances. So I use fusible web like Stitch Witchery to tack the seam allowances down before I turn the waistband. I cut pieces a little narrower than my seam allowance and twice the waistband width (see Fig. 69). After pressing the seams open, I put a piece of fusible web between the seam allowance and the garment on each side of the seam, and press again to fuse. With the waistband sewn and the elastic in, the web doesn't show, and inserting the elastic is much easier.

—Catherine Neff, Muscoda, WI

FIG. 69

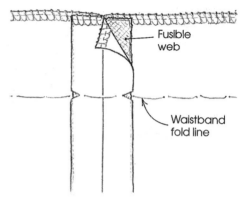

Fusible web

Waistband fold line

BULKLESS ELASTIC BINDING

To splice two pieces of elastic together without the bulk of an overlap, try the technique I use, as shown in Fig. 70: Cut a piece of twill tape the same width as the elastic and about 2 in. long, and place it underneath one end of the elastic. Stitch the overlap, using a multistitch zigzag set to your machine's widest width, and a short stitch length. Butt the other piece of elastic to the end of the first piece and zigzag again. Secure the edges of the butted elastic with another zigzag between the first two. Trim off the remaining twill tape. Your spliced elastic will slide beautifully within a casing.

—Andrea L. Moore, Spokane, WA

FIG. 70

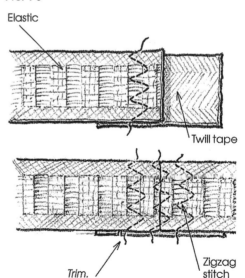

Elastic

Twill tape

Trim.

Zigzag stitch

FIG. 71

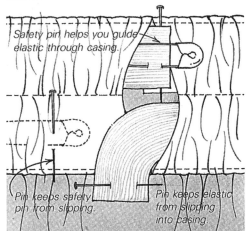

Safety pin helps you guide elastic through casing.

Pin keeps safety pin from slipping.

Pin keeps elastic from slipping into casing.

EASY ELASTIC

When inserting multiple rows of elastic, as at a waistline, the trick is to work all the elastic strips through their respective casings at the same time. If you try to work one through at a time, the casing will be so scrunched up that you won't be able to get the second, third, and fourth pieces of elastic through it.

Cut the elastic strips to the lengths you need to fit the waist, plus a ½-in. overlap. Attach a safety pin to one end of each strip and a straight pin to the other, perpendicular to the length. Insert the elastic pieces one at a time, safety pin first, into their casings (Fig. 71). The straight pin will keep the elastic from slipping into the casing as you work it through. Work ½ in. of each elastic strip into its casing at a time, thereby keeping the pieces nearly even and scrunching up all the casings at the same time.

Here's another hint: If one of the safety pins slips backward as you work the other elastic pieces through, put a straight pin into the casing between the two prongs of the safety pin, then up under one of them at an angle. Keep adjusting the positions of the straight pins as you push the elastic along. Once all the elastic strips are through their casings, overlap and pin the ends of each one with a safety pin. Try on the garment for size. Safety pins hold better than straight pins, and they won't stick you when you slip into the garment.
—*Marsha Stein, Waterbury, CT*

ADJUSTABLE ELASTIC

I do quite a bit of long-distance sewing for relatives and friends and prefer patterns that require little or no fitting. Many of these have elastic waistbands and, for children's garments, elastic cuffs. To make the final adjustment as trouble-free as possible, I make the elastic adjustable. On the inside of the casing I make a buttonhole the same width as the elastic, as shown in Fig. 72. I thread the elastic through this buttonhole, and I mail the garment with the ends of the elastic pulled out through the buttonhole and pinned with a safety pin. The recipient can adjust the elastic, sew the ends together, and simply allow the elastic to slip in through the buttonhole, leaving a finished look with no other sewing to be done. The buttonhole also makes later adjustments or replacing the elastic easy to do.
—*Suzanne Nesmith, Monett, MO*

FIG. 72

Casing

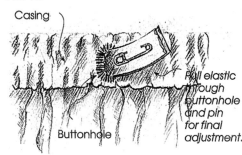

Buttonhole

Pull elastic through buttonhole and pin for final adjustment.

GATHERING WITH A GUIDE

If you need to gather to a specific measure, create a guide out of a strip of twill tape and a pull tab: Measure and cut a piece of cotton twill the length you need and attach it to a 1-in. by 2-in. pull tab with a few machine stitches. Fold the twill tape out of the way, and butt the side edge of the tab to the starting edge of the fabric to be gathered. Start the gathering stitches on the tab, continuing onto the fabric. Be sure not to

FIG. 73

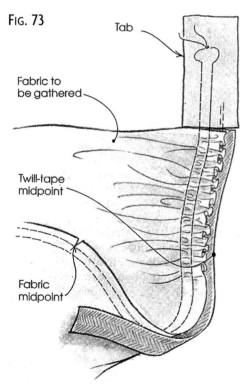

Tab

Fabric to
be gathered

Twill-tape
midpoint

Fabric
midpoint

stitch into the twill tape. (The fabric will overlap the twill tape.) At the tab, tie off the top threads and pull the bobbin threads to gather the fabric to the length of the tape (Fig. 73).

—*Mae M. Conner, Daytona Beach, FL*

LINING PATCH POCKETS

To make an easy and professional-looking patch pocket, line it. It will look and feel good each time you put your hand into it.

Fold 1 in. or more of the top of the pocket to the wrong side to make a self-facing. To make the lining, cut a small piece of fabric, compatible with the garment fabric, to the shape of the folded pocket, leaving ¼ in. at the top for the seam allowance.

With right sides together, stitch the self-facing to the lining with a ¼-in. seam allowance. Press the seam open.

Next, fold the pocket at the fold line of the self-facing (Fig. 74). Pin or baste the lining and pocket together about 1 in. from the raw edges.

Stitch around the pocket, leaving a 2-in. opening at the bottom. Turn the pocket right side out. Baste the lining and pocket, including the 2-in. opening. Press the pocket smooth, place it on the garment, and topstitch, securing the beginning and ending stitches.

The pocket and lining can sometimes be made of the same fabric, depending on the fabric weights. Cut the pocket and lining as one

FIG. 74

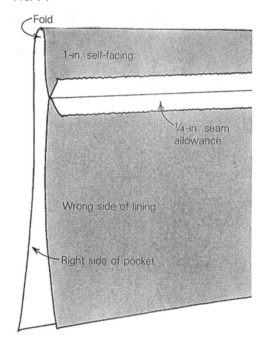

Fold

1-in. self-facing

¼-in. seam
allowance

Wrong side of lining

Right side of pocket

piece, fold it at the center, right sides together, and baste it. Close the pocket and attach it as described above.

—*Shirley Kates, Newtown, CT*

MATCHING FABRIC ACROSS POCKETS

If you want your patch-pocket fabric and garment fabric to line up, try this: Place the pocket pattern piece on the garment where the pocket is to be stitched, and trace the printed fabric design on it. (If you don't want to deface your pocket pattern or you need to do more than one pocket, trace the pattern onto tissue paper first.) Match the design traced on the pocket pattern piece with the fabric and cut out the pocket. If your garment is cut on the fold and you want two pockets opposite each other, fold the fabric

like the garment. Place the pocket pattern on the fabric and cut both layers at once for perfectly matched pockets.

—*Mrs. Gerald Tubbs, Penn Yan, NY*

BETTER BOUND POCKETS

When making bound or double-welt pockets in heavier fabrics, it's often difficult to get a smooth finish on the ends of the opening. The fabric refuses to roll under properly, making the welts pucker. If you can adjust the needle position of your machine, try my new way of stitching the ends: After stitching the top welt, stop with the needle down and pivot the fabric 90° at the corner. Lift and move the needle to the inside of the seamline (one click on most machines) as shown in Fig. 75. (If your machine doesn't allow you to offset the needle, lift the

FIG. 75

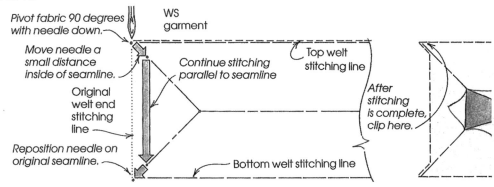

Pivot fabric 90 degrees with needle down.

Move needle a small distance inside of seamline.

Original welt end stitching line

Reposition needle on original seamline.

WS garment

Continue stitching parallel to seamline

Top welt stitching line

After stitching is complete, clip here.

Bottom welt stitching line

needle and move the fabric to the left one stitch while turning the hand wheel to reposition the needle in the fabric.) I sew the end of the welt with the center marker of my presser foot, not the needle, following the seamline. One stitch short of the end, I raise the needle, return it to its normal position (on the seamline), lower it, and pivot. Sew the bottom welt, then repeat the needle-moving on the other end. When clipping the corners of the opening, snip into the tiny acute angles you have made.

This method not only lets the fabric roll under beautifully, hiding the seam, but is really faster and easier than sewing just the top and bottom of the welts and stitching across the triangles after clipping, as some people suggest.
—*Cecelia Schmieder, Greenfield, MA*

NO-TEAR POCKETS

Whenever I'm sewing inset pockets in clothing, I switch to a close, narrow zigzag stitch when sewing around the pocket itself. This stitch is flexible, and I have never had a pocket rip out.
—*Sharon Wildermann, Hill, NH*

AN EASY WAY TO MAKE A BIAS TUBE

Some time ago, I needed about 36 yd. of cording for a studio couch. The method I used really saved me some time. It's also good for cording on pillows, or wherever a bias strip is needed.

To make a bias tube, cut a perfect square from the fabric to be used. The larger your square, naturally, the more strips you'll get. For upholstering, for example, I'd suggest using a square of 45 in. (or the full width of your fabric).

Cut the square diagonally to make two triangles (see step 1 in Fig. 76). It might be a good idea to pin small pieces of paper to each edge and label them *af* until you get the hang of this. With right sides of the triangles together, sew a narrow seam along edges *a* and *e*, and press open, as shown in step 3.

Right sides together, bring sides *b* and *d* together, as shown in step 3. The amount you allow the tip of side *b* to extend beyond side *d* determines the width of the bias strip. For example, to make a 2-in.-wide strip, extend the tip of *b* so that there is a 2-in. extension of fabric beyond the seam on side *d*; side *b* will be 2 in. short of meeting side *d* at the opposite end of the tube. Sew sides *b* and *d* together, press the seam open, and the bias tube is complete. To cut the strips (step 4), begin where the fabric extends beyond the tube and cut around, as though you were peeling an apple.
—*Mrs. Tom Gerson, Stillwater, MN*

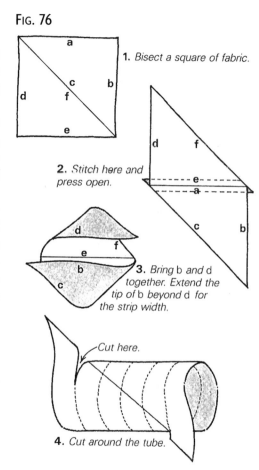

FIG. 76

1. *Bisect a square of fabric.*

2. *Stitch here and press open.*

3. *Bring b and d together. Extend the tip of b beyond d for the strip width.*

Cut here.

4. *Cut around the tube.*

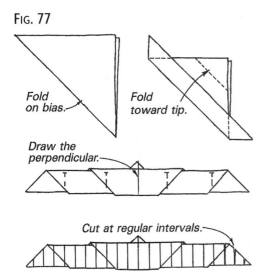

FIG. 77

Fold on bias.

Fold toward tip.

Draw the perpendicular.

Cut at regular intervals.

CUTTING BIAS STRIPS

Here is a way to cut bias strips that is less confusing and easier to remember than continuous-strip methods. Cut a square of fabric adequate for the bias strips you need. Fold it in half diagonally. Starting with the folded side, make folds toward the point, as shown in Fig. 77. Stop folding 1 in. or 1½ in. from the point, and pin to hold the folds in place. Draw a perpendicular line from the point to the outside edge of the folds. Starting from this line, draw lines at intervals that equal the width of the strip desired. With knife-edged scissors or a rotary cutter, cut on the lines drawn, and the strips are ready to be joined. To estimate the total length of your joined bias strip, figure the total length you'd get from your square of fabric if the strips were cut on the straight grain. You'll get a slightly shorter length when the strips are cut on the bias. In other words, you can get almost 12 ft. of 1-in. strips from a square foot of fabric.

—*Mary E. Weaver, Savannah, GA*

SEAMLESS PIPING

For fast, easy, stabilized piping, cut a bias strip of fabric the desired length and place it right side down on your ironing board. Cut strips of fusible webbing (such as Stitch Witchery) ¼ in. to ⅛ in. wide, and place them along the center of the bias strip. Then cut the piping filler 1 in.

longer than the bias strip and tie a simple knot in each end. Put pins in the knots, position the filler over the webbing, and use the pins to anchor it to the ironing board at the ends, as shown in Fig. 78. Lightly steam by holding your iron above the filler to begin the fusing process. Now fold the bias strip in half over the filler and press, keeping the edge of the iron in the crease formed by the filler thread. This seamless piping is very easy to apply precisely.

—*Frankie Leverett, Atlanta, GA*

FIG. 78

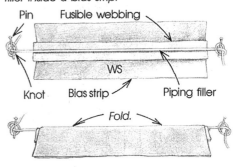

Use fusible webbing to seal piping filler inside a bias strip.

Pin   Fusible webbing

WS

Knot   Bias strip   Piping filler

Fold.

Iron along crease.

MAKING CORDED PIPING

To piece bias strips to make a length of corded piping, always sew the ends of the strips together along the straight grain of the fabric, as shown in drawing A in Fig. 79. The resulting small diagonal seam (see drawing C) will be relatively invisible and will allow the bias strip to stretch. Press the seam open and trim away the small protruding triangles (see drawing B), then proceed to add cording.

PERFECT LAPPED ZIPPERS

I've found that machine-stitching a lapped zipper often causes the fabric to shift, thereby distorting the grain and horizontal stripes. My method is very quick and neat: First close the seam, backstitching at the end of the opening. Then press the seam open, including the zipper seam allowances.

Inset the zipper on the right-hand seam allowance, leaving room for the tab to slide easily to the right of the seam. Baste it in place along the right seam allowance, as shown at left in Fig. 80. Now open the zipper, and machine-stitch with the zipper foot in the crease on the left-hand seam allowance. Start sewing from the top. When you near the zipper tab, lower the needle, raise the presser foot, and slide the tab up out of the way; then finish sewing. No stitching will show on the garment's right side.

Close the zipper, and remove the basting thread. Turn the skirt right side out, and pin the left side of the skirt to the left side of the zipper, slightly overlapping the fold, as shown at right in Fig. 80. With tiny backstitches sew by hand, about ⅜ in. from the fold, manipulating the grain or stripes to match the other side. On the very top I sometimes might move my line of stitching a little to the left to give the slide more room.

If I have fine fabric, like crepe de chine or charmeuse, I insert a narrow piece of organza or a similar suitable fabric before I sew to ensure a crisp look.

—*Charlotte Andrews, Haverford, PA*

FIG. 80

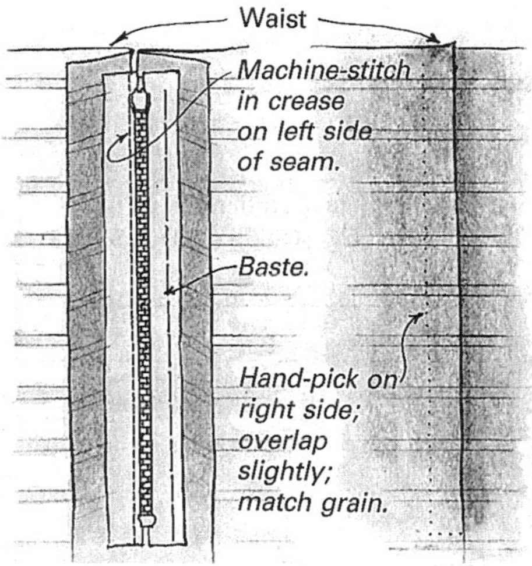

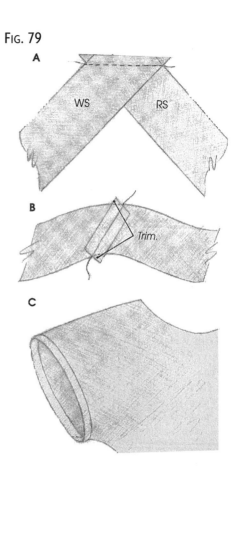

FIG. 79

A — WS, RS

B — Trim.

C

Waist

Machine-stitch in crease on left side of seam.

Baste.

Hand-pick on right side; overlap slightly; match grain.

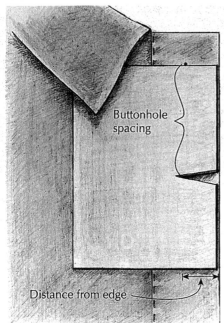

FIG. 81

Buttonhole spacing

Distance from edge

AN EASY WAY TO MARK BLOUSE BUTTONHOLES

It's easy to place and mark buttonholes on a fitted blouse if you use a template. You can make one out of an index card. First, find the fullest part of your bust (a button there will prevent the blouse from gaping), and mark this point on your pattern. Measure from the top buttonhole on your pattern to the new bust-point marking. Divide this measurement in half (or thirds if you prefer) to find the distance between your buttonholes. On the edge of an index card cut a notch that distance from one end. Make the point of the notch as deep as the distance you want the buttonhole to be from the edge of the blouse. Starting at the neckline, as shown in Fig. 81, position the edge of the card on the fold of your blouse opening and make a tiny dot at the notch point to mark one end of the next buttonhole. Then shift the end of the card to that dot to mark the next, and so on. Store the template in your pattern envelope for easy reference in the future.
—*Lucy Thompson, Livingston, TX*

BUTTON PLACEMENT GUIDES

The hole strips removed from the edges of computer paper are useful for marking button and snap placement as well as buttonholes. The holes on the paper strips are evenly spaced at ½-in. intervals. Place the computer strips along the line where snaps or buttons are to be placed and mark through the holes. The length of the strips can be extended by lining up the holes and joining the pieces with tape.
—*Andrea Moore, Spokane, WA*

FAKE BUTTONHOLE CLOSURE

Buttonholes in delicate or gauzy fabrics are nice, but they wear quickly. To save them, make fake buttonholes. Work the buttonholes, but don't cut them open. Sew a button on the top of each buttonhole and sew silk-covered snaps underneath. This also works well with fancy silk or antique buttons that are too fragile to button and unbutton.
—*Evelyn Blake, Roanoke, VA*

REMOVABLE BUTTON BAND

It's easy to make a closure on a reversible jacket so the jacket can be buttoned right over left when it's worn either side out. Just make a removable button band. Place buttonholes down both sides of the jacket front. Sew a row of shank buttons on a 1-in.-wide lined fabric band the length of the buttonholes, plus 1½ in. Button the band through the buttonholes on the left side of the jacket. The buttons are now in place to be buttoned traditionally.
—*Lucile Stutsman, Lincoln, CA*

REINFORCING BUTTONS ON SILK

When a silk jacquard or crepe de chine blouse or dress pattern requires a button placement with only fabric to support the button, I use heavy-weight, non-fusible interfacing rather than a backing button (Fig. 82). For small buttons, I cut out a tiny circle with a paper hole punch. For larger buttons, I use the top or bottom of my thimble or a thread spool to draw a circle on the interfacing scrap and then cut it out with small, sharp scissors. This reinforcement is strong, flexible, comfortable, and launderable.
—*Barbara Nachtigall, Roslindale, MA*

FIG. 82

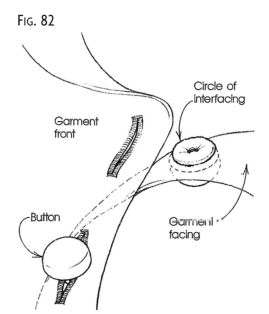

Circle of interfacing

Garment front

Button

Garment facing

SERGING THE EASE OUT OF CURVED HEMS

To avoid those diagonal tucks when casing the extra fabric on a shirttail or other circular hem, first serge the raw edge of the hem, wrong side up, using a three-thread stitch. Tighten the needle tension just a little to make the raw edge cup inward. Turn up the hem, steam lightly into place, and topstitch (Fig. 83).
—*T. R. Kelley, Junction City, OR*

EVEN A-LINE HEMS

To adjust the fullness of the hem on an A-line skirt evenly, first pin the hem. Then cut a length of seam binding that is long enough to travel around the top of the hem and overlap slightly where the two ends of the binding meet. Pin the seam binding to the hem while easing the fullness of the skirt fabric.

Machine-stitch the seam binding to the hem, stretching the binding between the pins. As you stretch, hold the binding in front of, and behind, the needle to avoid putting pressure on the needle. After it's stitched, the binding will resume its normal length and gather in the fullness of the hem as it does so. On a very wide A-line skirt, run a basting thread in the hem and gather the hem slightly to take up the ease first.
—*Ruth S. Galpin, Southport, CT*

FIG. 83

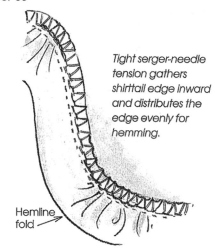

Tight serger-needle tension gathers shirttail edge inward and distributes the edge evenly for hemming.

Hemline fold

FIG. 84

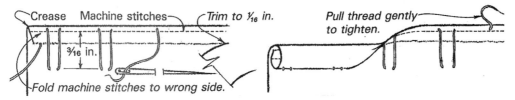

Crease   Machine stitches   Trim to ¹⁄₁₆ in.

Pull thread gently to tighten.

³⁄₁₆ in.

Fold machine stitches to wrong side.

FIG. 85

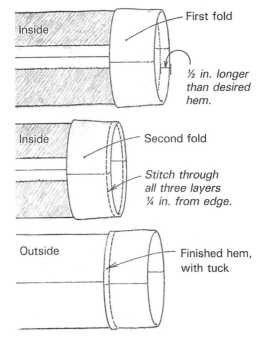

Inside — First fold

½ in. longer than desired hem.

Inside — Second fold

Stitch through all three layers ¼ in. from edge.

Outside — Finished hem, with tuck

HAND-ROLLED HEMS

I have a variation on the hand-rolled hem technique of designer Charles Kleibacker. The difference is that this method has hidden stitches.

Machine-stitch ¼ in. from the raw edge of the fabric, and trim the edge to within ¹⁄₁₆ in. of the stitching. Fold about 1 in. to 2 in. of the stitching to the wrong side, with the crease just inside the stitches, as shown in Fig. 84, finger-pressing as you go.

Insert the needle into the turned edge, bringing the thread out on the crease. Now insert the needle into the single layer of fabric directly opposite, picking up one to two threads. The stitches must be perpendicular to the edge of the hem, not slanted. Reinsert the needle through the creased edge, and let it travel inside ¼ in. before coming out again to repeat the process. And now for the magical part: After taking four to five stitches, bring the needle out at the edge of the crease and pull the thread gently to tighten and enclose the row of stitches. You will have a tightly rolled hem with all the stitches inside.
—*Tricia Klein, San Luis Obispo, CA*

AN EASY HEM

Here's a quick and bulkless hem that has served me well for years on short sleeves, shorts, toddlers' clothes, and even some styles of pants. Turn the garment to be hemmed inside out, and turn up a hem, as shown in Fig. 85, with the fold about ½ in. longer than you will want the finished length. Then fold over the same size hem once more, straighten the edges carefully, and press the bottom edge. Your hem is now three layers thick. Stitch ¼ in. away from the edge, catching all three layers. Turn the garment right side out and unfold the hem. You will have a neat hem with a decorative tuck that looks like a cuff. You can adjust the size of the cuff by adjusting the size of the folds you make, and the length taken up in the tuck is twice the width of the seam you sew.
—*B. Randy Johnstone, La Luz, NM*

MITERED CORNERS

For neat hemming on square corners, try mitered corners. It helps to practice with paper first, before using cotton broadcloth, poplin, or muslin. First, press fold lines at the hem depth, allowing them to cross at the corner, as shown in Fig. 86A. Then, using the cross as a guide point, fold the corner to the inside (Fig. 86B), and press the diagonal fold. On fabrics that

66

FIG. 86A

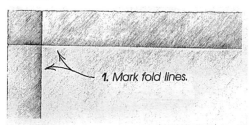

1. Mark fold lines.

FIG. 86B

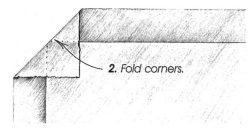

2. Fold corners.

FIG. 86C

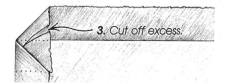

3. Cut off excess.

FIG. 86D

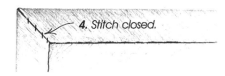

4. Stitch closed.

won't show a pressed crease easily, you may need to thread-trace the lines. Cut off the corner, leaving a generous seam allowance outside the diagonal fold line, then fold the two hemlines to the wrong side once more (Fig. 86C). The diagonal crease should fold at the center, making the two halves meet in a miter. Adjust the folds as necessary at the ironing board.

Finish the raw edges of the hem by turning them under or binding them. Now, to stitch the inner miter seam, turn the hem inside out. With right sides together, match the halves of the diagonal fold line and machine stitch in the crease. Turn the miter right side out and finish stitching the hem, either by hand or machine.

With heavy fabrics, it may be easier and more accurate to hand stitch the mitered corner from the outside. Wax a single strand of thread and run it under a hot iron to melt the wax. Use this waxed thread to slipstitch the miter (Fig. 86D).

ASYMMETRIC MITERS

With my method, any two hemmed edges coming together at a corner can be neatly mitered. The hems may vary in size and the seam need not be at a 45° angle to the edges, but the miter will be perfect, as shown in Fig. 87.

Press the fabric along the hemlines, and clean finish the cut edges by turning them under or zigzagging. Mark the intersection of the hems with pins or clips (step 1). Open the hems and fold the fabric right sides together, matching the two pins as shown in step 2. Stitch from the pins to where the hem creases intersect at the fabric fold; press the seam open on a point presser.

Turn the miter right side out, refold the hems, and flatten the excess fabric inside the hem corner as shown (step 3). Press. You may trim the excess fabric after pressing the corner, but be sure you don't need it for weight in the corner. Also be certain you'll never want to adjust the garment's length, because once the corner is trimmed, it is no longer possible to lengthen it.
—*Shirley McKeown, Adelphi, MD*

FIG. 87

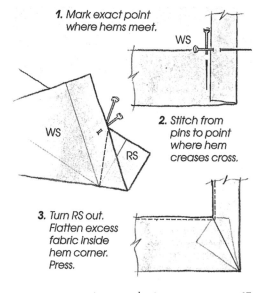

1. Mark exact point where hems meet.

WS

2. Stitch from pins to point where hem creases cross.

WS

RS

3. Turn RS out. Flatten excess fabric inside hem corner. Press.

Chapter 5

PRESSING

TAILOR'S PRESSING TOOLS

Two traditional tailoring notions are a dauber for dampening limited areas, like seams, and a sleeve pad, which slips into awkward places to simplify pressing. Most tailors make these tools for themselves.

A dauber is a strip of soft or medium woolen cloth about 3½ in. wide, and long enough to roll tightly into a cylinder about 1 in. thick. The long edges should be unfinished. After rolling it up, whip the dauber closed with a strong thread. One dauber should last you a lifetime, and it will get better (and more ragged looking) with use. Simply dip it into water and wipe it along the area you want to press.

Pressing pads of various shapes can be made to augment the press buck, the tailor's primary pressing aid. The one I find most useful is about 13 in. long and tapers from 6 in. wide at one end to 4½ in. wide at the other. The ends should be rounded. Cut enough layers of an old woolen blanket in this shape to make about a ¾-in. stack. Fasten the layers loosely together with a few stab stitches, and cover the whole thing in a smooth cotton or heavy lining rayon. This is a big help for pressing sleeve heads, sleeve hems, and elbow seams.
—*Stanley Hostek, Seattle, WA*

SEAM ROLL

A seam roll (Fig. 88) is a firm, sawdust-filled, cylindrical pressing aid used to open seams, especially in narrow areas like sleeves and trouser legs. One surface is usually wool, the other canvas; a rolled towel in a tube sock will substitute.

LONG SEAM ROLL

My local lumber company carries a perfect seam roll that's long enough so you can press pants seams open without having to move them. It's a 3-ft. to 4-ft. length of 1½-in.-dia. stair railing. The railing is nice and round on the top, so seam allowances don't press through to the garment; and the bottom is flat, so it stays put on the ironing board. Select a smooth piece of rail; the only finishing is gluing felt to the cut ends.
—*Mrs. T. VanderMolen, Grand Rapids, MI*

POINT PRESSER

The point presser, or edge board (Fig. 89) is a multipurpose tool. The top is positioned underneath seams when pressing them open, so the edges of the seam allowances don't imprint on the face of the garment; the pointed end is for reaching seams in tight places, like collars, lapel points, and the points of welts and flaps. The wooden base serves as a clapper for holding steamed and pressed edges flat while they cool and dry after the iron is removed.

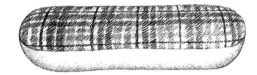

FIG. 88

FIG. 89

SLEEVE BOARD AS SEAM PRESSER

If you've got a sleeve board, you don't need to buy an additional tool for pressing open seams or bother with laying strips of paper under the seam allowances. Just lay your sleeve board on its side and press the seams open on the padded edge of the board. Most sleeve boards are very stable on their sides and longer than typical seam boards.
—*Andrea L. Moore, Spokane, WA*

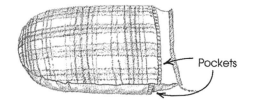

FIG. 90

Pockets

TAILOR'S MITT

A tailor's mitt is used to protect your hand while patting a hot, steamed surface. The softly stuffed mitt has a pocket on each side (see Fig. 90) into which a hand can slip. Many sewing stores sell inexpensive mitts. The mitt is also a handy surface for pressing the curve of a collar band.

OVEN-MITT PRESSING AID

You can make a great tool for pressing seams open in hard-to-reach areas out of an oven mitt. Start with a mitt covered with silvered fabric if possible, for the greatest protection from steam. Cover the mitt with three or four layers of cotton terry toweling (I use old, stained, but not much worn hand towels), cut and sewn in the shape of the original mitt, each mitt layer about ¼ in. larger than the previous layer. After the last mitt layer has been put on, your hand should just be able to squeeze into the mitt, and you should still be able to manipulate your hand so you can support almost any small, awkward shape while you press with the other hand. I find the thumb particularly handy, especially for children's clothes and when I want to use just the tip or edge of the iron on delicate fabrics. If your mitt has silver on one side only, be sure to mark that side of the new mitt so you can use that side when you're steam pressing.
—*Sharon Cirrito, Niagara Falls, NY*

TIME-SAVING TRICKS FOR PRESSING

You can simplify pressing on dresses and blouses with elastic waists or wrists if you attach a drawstring to each end of the elastic. Make it long enough to loosen the gathers until the fabric is flat for pressing; then draw it up and tie a loop knot for wearing. When you're sewing a blouse, if you make the sleeve plackets extra long, ironing will be much easier.

Pants creases and pleats will stay sharp if you baste them in before washing. Remove the basting threads after drying and pressing. Wool pants are also easier to press without the linings. Turn the lining into long underwear to wear with the pants by putting elastic in the waist. Or loosen the lining at the hem for easier pressing.
—*Susan Herrmann, Damascus, OH*

PRESSING A FOLD

Whenever you need to press a fold on any cloth, don't mark the foldline. Instead, mark where the folded edge will meet. You won't have to worry about burned fingers or hard-to-see marks; just fold the edge to the marked line, and press.
—*Martha Fee, Centerport, NY*

AVOID LEAVING HEM IMPRESSIONS

A strip of brown paper placed between the fabric layers of a hem before pressing them prevents the hemline from leaving a press line on the right side of the garment.
—*Susan L. Wiener, Spring Hill, FL*

SPRAY STARCH IN THE SEWING ROOM

One of my most valuable sewing aids is spray starch. Lots of starch adds body even to whisper-thin cottons and silk (yes, I starch silk—scandalous, isn't it?), enabling me to sew them as easily as kettle-cloth. Whenever I press, I starch.

I begin by starching and pressing my pre-washed fabric before I cut it. Heavy starch minimizes cutting distortion and helps the grain line stay true. During construction, starch boosts the power of the iron and can even replace pins, particularly when pinning distorts, as in machine-stitched invisible hems. For narrow top-stitched hems and edges, I machine-baste along the fold line, trim the allowance, and fold the cut edge once to the basting and again along the basting. Then I squirt it with starch. Starch lets me turn a $1/8$-in. edge around an armhole neatly and painlessly, with no pins or hand-basting.

Starching open seam allowances and darts helps to stick them in place, preventing them from folding or bunching up under intersecting seams. Narrow French seams don't shift if starched crisp and neat before sewing. Starched flat-felled seams are perfect every time. Spray starch is also good for taming pleats and coercing facings into folding under. There is one drawback, though: Starch messes up the soleplate of your iron. I use a commercial iron cleaner like Clean and Glide.
—*Leslie McElderry, Theodore, AL*

IRONING COTTON OR LINEN

Before ironing a difficult or delicate linen or cotton garment, mist the surface evenly with water. Roll the item up, place it in a plastic bag, and put it in the freezer for a few hours or overnight. Like magic the iron will glide easily across the crisp, cold surface.
—*Karen Grille, East Cambridge, MA*

CLEANING A SCORCHED IRON

The grimy build-up of fusible web and new fabric finishes on the soleplate of an iron can be removed with WD-40, a lubricant sold in most hardware stores. Spray some on a piece of absorbent cotton or paper towel and use the towel to clean the cool iron. After cleaning the plate, wipe off any excess lubricant. Heat the iron to a low temperature and iron over a clean paper towel until the plate is thoroughly clean.
—*Princesa Alexander, Henrietta, TX*

PRESS CLOTHS

I use my grandmother's cotton batiste handkerchiefs as press cloths. Moisture is distributed evenly, and their semi-transparency makes them easy to position over seamlines. Tattered edges have no effect on their performance.
—*Mary Elliott, Milwaukee, WI*

DISPOSABLE PRESS CLOTHS

After using nonwoven fabric-softener sheets such as Bounce or Snuggle in the dryer, I recycle them as press cloths for small craft projects. These nearly transparent sheets can withstand the high heat settings needed to set fabric paint or double-fuse materials such as Wonder Under. I place one or two sheets under and over my designs before pressing to protect both the iron and ironing surface; should any glitter or iridescent particles from the paint or fusible materials adhere to the sheets, I just throw the sheets away.
—*Barbara Nachtigall, Roslindale, MA*

PESKY IRON CORDS

To keep the iron's electrical cord out of the way, insert a hook into the ceiling directly over the ironing board. Looping the cord through the hook gets it up, away from the fabric. You will probably need an extension cord because of the extra height.
—*Sue Hodgson, Ferguson, MO*

MANAGING YARDAGE WHEN PRESSING

When I complained about the fabric falling to the floor when I press preshrunk yardage, my local dry cleaner shared this trick with me: Put a long cardboard tube (you can probably scavenge one from your fabric store—the bigger the diameter of the tube, the better) on a table or chair in front of the ironing board, and as you press the fabric, carefully roll it onto the tube. This keeps it unwrinkled and ready to use until you're ready to cut it.
—*Toni Toomey, Eugene, OR*

PROFESSIONAL-STYLE IRONING-BOARD COVER

Here's how to make an ironing-board cover that will surely improve the quality of your pressing efforts. The cover has the same layers of padding as the chest-boards used by professional tailors. I used a standard ironing-board cover as a pattern, allowing additional space for the thickness of the padding on the top layer that holds the whole thing together with a drawstring edge.

For the top, use a brushed twill-weave cotton called moleskin placed fuzzy side down. This wicks the moisture from steam away from the pressing surface. Make several of these cotton covers while you're at it so you will have a fresh one to use while a soiled cover is in the wash. For the middle layer, use ⅝-in.-thick knitted cotton padding, which also wicks moisture away and provides a soft surface for pressing. Many tailoring and dry-cleaning supply companies carry both moleskin and knitted cotton. For the bottom layer, use two or three layers of felted wool for more padding and for a final, quicker-drying material to wick the last of the moisture away. Wash old wool blankets (or remnants) several times in hot water to felt them.

This may seem like a lot of trouble for an ironing-board cover, until you consider the cost of the fine fabrics you work with and hours you spend pressing as you sew. The final justification will be in the results. You'll love them!
—*Zulema Anté, Houston, TX*

EASY IRONING-BOARD COVER REPAIR

If your ironing-board cover accidentally rips and you need a temporary repair, iron a piece of fusible interfacing over the wound. It lasts a long time, and its thin edges won't affect pressing.
—*Norma Matthews, Sacramento, CA*

A PORTABLE, LIGHTWEIGHT IRONING SURFACE

You can make an easy-to-grab, easy-to-store ironing board, great for quick jobs and pressing without leaving your machine, from the cardboard forms that fabric bolts come wrapped around. Your favorite fabric salesperson will probably be glad to give you an empty form. Cotton flannel, toweling, drill, and sheeting would all make serviceable covers. Here's how to cover the form: Measure a long strip of your covering material that's exactly as wide as the form, not including the ends, and that's long enough to wrap around it the way yardage would at least twice (more wouldn't hurt, if you've got the fabric). Before you cut, measure one more length that's about 3 in. wider on each end. Use the extra width to wrap around the ends, then handstitch the whole cover to itself, folding under the raw edges.
—*Pat Storla, Moscow, IN*

Chapter 6

HAND STITCHING

NEEDLES

The most commonly used needles for hand sewing are sharps and betweens (Fig. 91). Sharps have rounded eyes and come in medium lengths for general hand sewing. Betweens are shorter than sharps and better for making fine, short stitches. Many quilters recommend betweens for even quilting.

FIG. 91

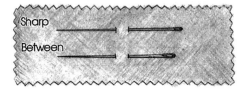

NO MORE DROPPED AND WAYWARD NEEDLES

If you're finding your hand-sewing needles easy to drop and hard to spot, try slipping your most-used ones into tiny, brightly colored pieces of nonraveling Ultrasuede even when they're in your pincushion and while you're threading them. They'll be much easier to handle, and they won't roll around on your table top.
—*Deborah C. Little, Alva, FL*

UNSTICKING NEEDLES

Here's an old trick from my diapering days. If your needle or pin seems sticky and won't go through fabric easily, run it through your hair once or twice. Just enough oil will be deposited on the needle to make sewing easier.
—*Martha F. Fee, Northport, NY*

TO THREAD A NEEDLE

This is a simple hint, but it makes threading needles much easier. Cut the thread on a slant. Hold the thread as close as possible to its cut end; hold the needle so that you easily see the eye (holding it up against a white background helps). Now push the eye of the needle over the thread, instead of pushing the thread into the eye. (If the thread is limp or frayed, try waxing where you cut.)
—*Mary E. Weaver, Savannah, GA*

THREADING

Thread a needle with the end of the thread that leads off the spool. Thread is spun so that this end will slip through the eye more easily than the other end.
—*Lois Morrison, Leonia, NJ*

QUILTER'S KNOT

A quilter's knot, also called a tailor's knot, is a secure, sturdy knot used to begin a line of stitching, even in slippery nylon thread. Thread a needle and hold it horizontally, pointing left, in your right hand. Hold the tail end of the thread behind the needle in your left hand with the end pointing toward the needle eye (lefties, reverse hand directions). Pinch the cut thread end to the shank of the needle with your right thumb and index finger, about ¾ in. down the shank. Then wrap the thread tightly around the shank toward the point four times, as shown in Fig. 92. Pinch these wraps with your right thumb and index finger and, with your left hand, pull the needle out from the pinching fingers toward the left.

FIG. 92

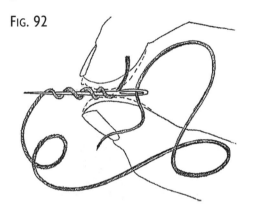

NO-WAX THREAD WAXING

Save your soap-bar remnants and use them to run your thread through for smooth, tangle-free hand sewing. The soap won't dry out and splinter as commercially sold beeswax eventually does, and you won't have to worry about wax stains. Besides, it costs nothing.
—*Martha McKeon, Sandy Hook, CT*

NEAT KNOTS

Here's a way to eliminate unsightly knots in double threads when you're sewing handwork or embroidering. Put both ends of the thread or floss through the needle's eye, as shown in step 1 of Fig. 93. Then pull the thread so that its looped end is longer. Make a stitch in the fabric in the direction in which you'll be stitching, and pull the needle through until the loop is al-

FIG. 93

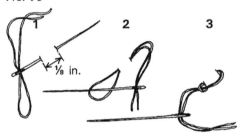

most at the point where you first inserted the needle into the fabric. Now put the point of the needle through the loop (step 2) and pull the thread until you have secured it (step 3).
—*Ilya Sandra Perlingieri, San Diego, CA*

THREAD TRACING

One secure way to mark grainlines and construction details on fabric is by thread-tracing them. On the right side of the fabric, stitch down the line to be marked using silk or basting thread. Make no knot in the thread, but fasten it at the beginning of the basting with a small backstitch. Take a long basting stitch, then a short stitch as shown in Fig. 94A; this makes a row of long stitches on the right side and small stitches on the wrong side.

You can use thread tracing to mark center lines, seamlines, fold lines, buttonholes, darts, and any other position marks on cut garment pieces. Thread tracing is also helpful in draping. By marking the lengthwise and crosswise grain on the uncut fabric, you can make sure you keep the grainlines straight as you drape the fabric on the body.

The following is the thread-tracing method draping instructor Suzanne Stern learned in the workrooms of Jacques Fath in the late 1940s.

Stern explains that they laid the muslin on which the pattern had been marked over the fashion fabric and carefully pinned the layers together exactly on top of all the seamlines and reference points. Turning the layers over so the fashion fabric was uppermost, they converted the pin markings to thread markings by stitching with a single contrasting thread and catching only the fashion fabric. "We stitched in a distinctive pattern of two short stitches, then one long one. In case we inadvertently caught the muslin layer, we left the knotted thread

ends at start and finish a little long so we could snip out the offending stitch and have some excess thread to draw up to knot the ends together.

"To keep our stitching line accurate, we would stretch a short length of the thread com-

FIG. 94A

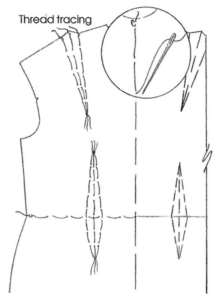

Thread tracing

FIG. 94B

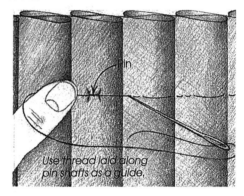

Use thread laid along
pin shafts as a guide.

ing from the previous marking stitch to the next pin. Then we stitched along the thread guide as if it were a ruler, as shown in Fig. 94B. When we reached the pin, we pulled up the thread and stretched it to the next pin."

FIG. 95

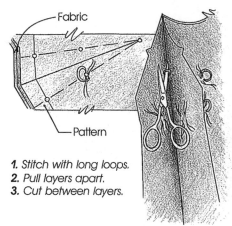

Fabric

Pattern

1. *Stitch with long loops.*
2. *Pull layers apart.*
3. *Cut between layers.*

TAILOR'S TACKS

Try tailor's tacks to mark sewing symbols, darts, and seams in fabric. Tacks don't leave traces, as a pencil or chalk might, and you can accurately mark two layers of fabric at once.

Thread a needle with a length of doubled thread that contrasts with the fabric. Make a slit with the needle point in the pattern tissue over the symbol to be marked. Through the slit, take a small stitch through both layers of fabric. Pull the thread until you have a 1-in. tail left, then take another stitch in the same place, as shown in Fig. 95. Leave a 1- to 2-in. loop, and cut the needle loose, leaving another 1-in. tail. Mark each symbol, then gently remove the pattern tissue. Pull the fabric layers apart carefully and snip the threads between layers, leaving the threads to mark your symbol or stitching line.

BASTING

Two excellent and secure methods of basting are tailor basting and cross stitch; both anchor the fabric layers together with stitches that run perpendicular to the direction of stress. To tailor-baste, take a stitch from right to left (left to right for left-handers), then move downward about an inch before starting the next stitch (see Fig. 96A).

Cross stitch is also worked from right to left, but moves sideways, as shown in Fig. 96B. Cross stitch forms a pattern of Xs, and when taken

only partway through the fabric so as to be invisible on the right side it is called catch stitch. Cross stitch for basting should penetrate all fabric layers and hold them securely.

FIG. 96A

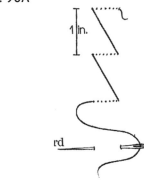

1 in.

rd

FIG. 96B

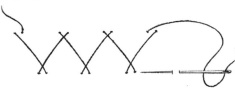

BASTING DIFFICULT FABRICS

Plain running stitches are sometimes not secure enough for slippery, stretchy fabrics, or for try-ons. Here's a strong alternative that goes in quickly and is easier to take out than back-stitches: Hand-baste the entire seam with a running stitch, but when you get to the end of the

seam, turn around and make running stitches of the same size along the entire seam in the opposite direction, filling in the gaps between the stitches you made the first time. I use lengths of tape laid against the seamline to provide a straightedge to guide my hand stitches, which in turn provide a guide for accurate machine stitching. Before basting, I'm careful to pin at right angles to the seam I'm going to stitch to avoid distortion while I'm basting.
—*Lonnie Piposzar, Pittsburgh, PA*

SLIP BASTING

To match plaids and stripes accurately, slip baste your seams before machine sewing. Press one seam allowance under on the seamline. Pin the folded edge over the second piece, right sides up, matching the seamlines (Fig. 97). Bring a threaded needle out of the fold, hiding the knot. Now take a ¼-in. stitch in the under fabric, then slip the needle into the fold for ¼ in. Repeat for the length of the seam. Use the basting

FIG. 97

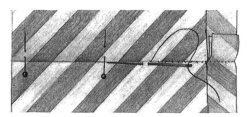

line on the wrong side of the fabric as a guide for machine stitching.

SLIPSTITCH

Slipstitch is a hemming technique used to join either two folded edges or one folded edge to flat fabric. You can work it from either the right or wrong side to produce a nearly invisible seam. Take small stitches alternately through one fold then the other, as shown in Fig. 98, or through the flat fabric and the folded edge, to bring the two close together. Don't pull the thread too tight, or the fabric will pucker.

BLINDSTITCH

A hemming blindstitch is hidden between the hem and the garment. Pick up just a few threads of the garment fabric, then a few of the hem, using a running stitch, as shown in Fig. 99A.

Blind catch stitch, which forms a network of little crosses, has more give than blind straight stitch. Because each stitch catches only one or a few threads, nothing shows on the right side of the garment.

Place the fabric layers wrong sides together and fold the top layer back to the depth where you'd like the stitching to be, as shown in Fig. 99B. Take a tiny stitch from right to left in the bottom layer of fabric if you're right-handed; reverse the directions if you're left-

FIG. 98

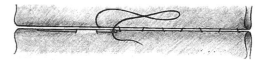

FIG. 99A

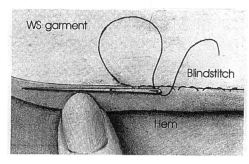

WS garment

Blindstitch

Hem

FIG. 99B

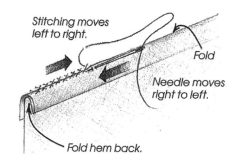

WS garment

Stitching moves left to right.

Fold

Needle moves right to left.

Fold hem back.

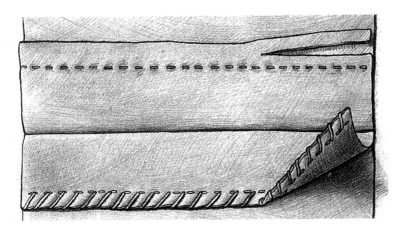

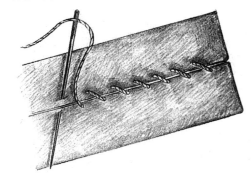

HAND OVERCASTING

To hand-overcast a seam allowance, which provides a smooth, flat seam finish and prevents raveling, first press the seam open. Stitch ¼ in. from each raw edge and trim to ⅛ in. Overcast the edge by hand, sewing from either end of the seam and taking evenly spaced diagonal stitches that wrap over the edge, as shown in Fig. 100A. Repeat for the other seam allowance. If the fabric ravels easily, make the stitches deeper and closer together.

You can also use overcasting to join two edges that are butted together, as shown in Fig. 100B, and you can overcast the cut edges of braid to prevent raveling.

PAD STITCHING

Pad stitching is used by tailors to fasten interfacing in place, add body to the garment, and shape curved areas like the collar and lapels. When done by hand, pad stitching consists of rows of slanting stitches worked with a single strand of matching thread. Pad stitching is a permanent part of your garment, so the stitches should be taken through the interfacing and only partway through the garment fabric; they shouldn't show through the fabric.

Insert the needle in the fabric slightly to the side of the beginning point for the first stitch, leaving the knot of the thread on the surface, as

handed. Move to the right, and take another stitch, again from right to left, in the fold of the upper layer of fabric. Keep moving to the right, alternating stitching in the bottom and top layers until you've stitched all the way across or around the edge.

EVEN HEMSTITCHING

Hem stitching that is too tight will cause puckers, and stitching that is too loose will cause sags. To make neat handsewn hems, fold the hem to the appropriate length, and pin and press it. Then pin the fabric to a small pillow. With the pillow on your lap, hand-stitch toward yourself, keeping the fabric taut. This will keep your stitches even.

—*Ellen Maurer, Boulder, CO*

shown in Fig. 101. Curve the fabric layers over your hand while pad stitching to help shape the garment. Take successive slanted stitches to the bottom of the row, then a longer stitch to put the needle in position for the next row. Do not turn the work. The second row is worked upward, parallel to the first row. Only your hands move up and down as you stitch; the work is never turned.

FIG. 101

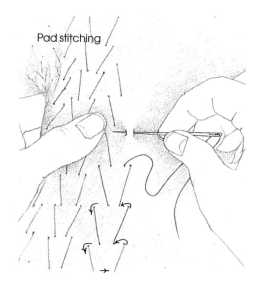

Pad stitching

The smaller and closer together the stitches, the more body and stiffness they impart. Different stitch lengths and spacings are appropriate for different fabrics and in different areas within a garment. The stitches in the outer areas of the undercollar need to be closer than in the center, for example. Experiment with the density of the stitches before you begin the actual stitching.

FELL STITCHING

Fell stitches are small, vertical hand stitches that are nearly invisible on both sides of the fabric. Designer Mary McFadden uses fell stitching to anchor the folded seam allowance of bias corded piping to the inside of garment edges.

Secure the knot inside the fold, working from right to left. Insert the needle straight above the last stitch in the fold into the fabric beneath it, picking up a tiny stitch. Bring the needle diagonally underneath the fold and emerge a short distance away, as shown in Fig. 102. Space your stitches from ⅟₁₆ to ⅜ in. apart, closer for slippery fabrics or for a stronger seam.

HANDPICKING

Handpicking adds a line of textured hand-stitched dots, each a soft pucker, to an otherwise smooth surface of fabric such as gabardine. The backstitches used for handpicking, sewn as shown in Fig. 103, won't pull out like straight stitches. Handpicking can be done with regular sewing thread, slightly heavier thread such as a buttonhole twist, or with embroidery floss. The stitches catch only the top layer(s) of fabric and

FIG. 102

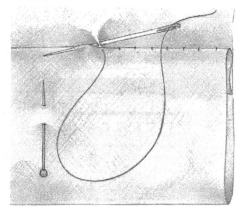

FIG. 103

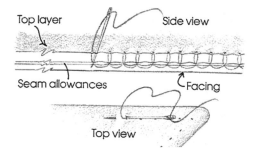

Top layer — Side view

Seam allowances — Facing

Top view

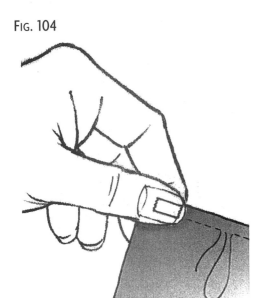

FIG. 104

don't show on the underside. For perfect hand-picking, keep the stitches spaced evenly and catch the same number of threads in each stitch. Handpicking is easier to do before the detail, such as a collar, has been completed so you can still put your fingers between the layers.

The effect of handpicking can be varied by increasing the length of the stitches (you can catch four or five threads rather than one or two), and by increasing the layers of fabric caught by the stitches (top layer and seam allowances, instead of just the top layer).

A FINGERTIP SEAM GAUGE

Eyeballing a seam you're hand-stitching isn't always accurate enough, especially when you're doing precision piecing, but marking every seamline is very time-consuming. My solution is to stick a ¼-in.-wide piece of masking tape to the thumbnail of the hand that holds the pieces being sewn, as shown in Fig. 104. It's easy to line up the edge of the fabric with the outside edge of the tape and to use the inside edge as a moving marker for your stitches. Some quilting sources sell ¼-in.-wide tape for marking entire seamlines. I use the tape for its width and only need a tiny length for a day's worth of stitching instead of as much tape as every seam I can sew. And this method is much faster than sticking down all that tape to the fabric.

—*Terry Grant, Ashland, OR*

SWING TACK

A swing tack anchors two fabric layers together while allowing some freedom for them to move separately, as on the hems of lining and garment, or when attaching a shoulder pad.

To make a swing tack, take a small stitch invisibly through one edge of the garment, then another through the edge of the lining or pad. Leave a ½- to 1-in. slack in the thread. Repeat this long stitch several times, keeping the slack even. Then work closely spaced blanket stitches over the threads to cover and reinforce them, as shown in Fig. 105.

FIG. 105

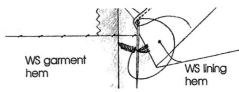

WS garment hem

WS lining hem

ULTRASTRONG, PERFECTLY MATCHED THREADS

Dental floss makes a nearly unbreakable thread for sewing on buttons and hooks, but it's pretty ugly. If you unravel a few threads from the straight or cross grain of your fashion fabric and thread them on a needle, you can use them to cover up the white dental floss.

—*Evelyn R. Blake, Roanoke, VA*

BUTTONS THAT STAY ON

I've been sewing buttons on for over 50 years and have never had a button come off. The secret? No knot!

To begin sewing the button on, stitch the thread three or four times through the fabric where the center of the button will be. Don't tie a knot. Then sew on the button. If the button has no shank, put a pin on top of the button under the first thread you've sewn through it. You need to sew through the button's holes just three or four times. Remove the pin, and wrap the thread around the "shank" you've made between the garment and button. Catch the thread securely on the underside of the garment, clip it, and the button is on to stay.

—Ann Estey, Boulder, CO

BUTTONS IN HALF THE TIME

Sewing buttons onto a garment goes twice as fast if you fold the thread in half and pull the folded end through the needle's eye until the folded and free ends meet. Now you can sew with four threads instead of two. Leave a long tail on the underside of the garment, sew through each pair of holes in the button twice, and knot securely on the back. The button will be as strongly attached as if you had sewn through each pair of holes eight times with a single strand.

—Mary Applegate, Hershey, PA

SEWING ON SNAPS

Years ago, when I worked for Mainbocher, we used to call the two parts of the snap the male and female. Sew the male part first and, to make sure it doesn't rip off, use a buttonhole stitch. Rub some chalk on the male part of the snap. When you press the fabric down on it, you'll have a little dot of chalk right where the female part is to be stitched.

—Lee Pecora, Massapequa Park, NY

PRECISION PLACEMENT FOR HOOKS AND EYES

Here's how to position the eyes of a hook-and-eye set precisely: First sew on the hook, then lap the garment as you want it to be when the closure is complete, pinning it in that position. Slip the eye onto the hook, then pin through the holes at each side of the eye, attaching the eye to the underlap so that it doesn't distort either layer, or offset them at their upper or lower edges. Take a few stitches to secure the eye before unpinning.

—Andrea Moore, Spokane, WA

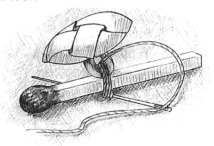

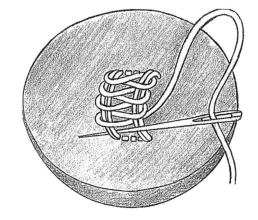

THREAD SHANKS

Sewng a wrapped thread shank for a button raises the button above the surface of the garment so that when closed, the button will rest on top of the buttonhole instead of sinking into the buttonhole and distorting its shape. A thread shank beneath a button is especially needed on heavy and bulky fabrics and can be added to sew-through buttons as well as to those with a built-in shank.

To make a thread shank, first sew on the button as usual, placing a finger, a couple of pins, or a wooden matchstick under the button to raise it above the surface. On the last stitch, bring the thread through the button only, then wind the thread tighty around the stitches for several wraps, as shown in Fig. 106A. Fasten securely on the underside of the garment.

To add a thread shank to the back of a fabric or needle-lace button, take two long stitches on the back of the button, parallel to each other; repeat. Weave back and forth across the threads as shown in Fig. 106B: over one side, down between the threads, and under the other side. Repeat until the thread lengths are completely covered, then tie off and cut the thread.

You can also use the buttonhole stitch to make a shank for the back of a thread-covered button. At the center back, stitch several parallel loops of thread. Starting at one end, cover the loops evenly with buttonhole stitches, as shown in Fig. 106C.

KEYHOLE BUTTONHOLE

To make a handworked keyhole buttonhole, start by marking the length and position on the right side of the garment with chalk or thread. Outline the buttonhole with short machine stitches, then slash from the narrow end toward the keyhole, inside the stitching. Snip from the end of the slash toward the stitching as shown in Fig. 107, and trim the keyhole circle to about ⅛ in. in diameter.

Use heavy-duty or buttonhole twist thread to edge the buttonhole. Note that in the buttonhole stitch, the needle crosses the working thread twice, forming a row of picots on the edge of the buttonhole.

Start at the end farthest from the keyhole. Bring your needle up ⅛ in. from the edge of the slash (on the left side, if you are right-handed), hiding your knot between the facing and the fashion fabric. Work up the left side of the slash to the keyhole, making the stitches deep enough to cover the machine stitching, and close together but not touching.

In the keyhole, the stitches are close together at the edge but fan out around the circle. Take several long stitches across the end of the slash. Cover these threads with buttonhole stitches, (catching the fabric under the threads in the stitching) to reinforce the end with a bar tack.

FIG. 107

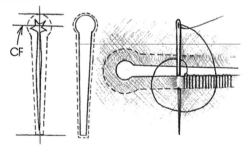

THREAD EYES

In fine dressmaking, thread eyes are usually used where fasteners might show. You can make thread eyes (or belt loops) by finger-crocheting or doing the buttonhole stitch over several threads.

Fig. 108 shows how to finger-crochet a simple chain stitch.

Use a double thread about 20 in. long (for a 1½-in. chain) with a knot at the end. Make a tiny stitch to secure the thread. Make another stitch, ending with the needle on the right side of the garment, and leave about a 3-in. loop (a).

Transfer the needle to your left hand (if you are right-handed). Hold the needle and garment firmly. With your other hand, catch the long end of the thread and pull it through the loop to form a second loop (b). Pull the thread until the first loop is tight (c).

Continue until the chain is long enough to suit your purpose. Then bring the needle through the last loop and pull it tight to lock the stitch (d). Put the needle through the garment where needed, making a few small stitches to fasten the chain securely.

—*Shirley Kates, Newtown, CT*

FIG. 108

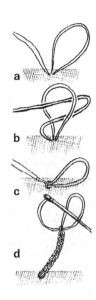

a

b

c

d

Chapter 7

❖

MACHINE STITCHING

EASY MACHINE-NEEDLE THREADING

Do you thread your sewing machine needle front to the back? You can make the needle eye more visible and easier to thread by painting the presser foot directly behind the needle with white nail polish or typing correction fluid such as Liquid Paper. The white background will reflect light.

—*Evelyn Blake, Roanoke, VA*

TANGLE-FREE BOBBINS

When winding thread onto a sewing-machine bobbin, hold tightly to a 3-in. thread tail that you draw through the hole in the top of the bobbin. If the thread doesn't break at the edge of the hole after a few revolutions, trim it and continue winding. This eliminates a loose tail to catch in the bobbin race as the bobbin unwinds.

—*Beverly Stone, Encinitas, CA*

AN EASY START FOR SEAMS

If you're working with fabric that needs help starting through your machine, just pull gently on the needle and bobbin threads to guide the fabric until you can grasp it.

—*Marge Pfeil, Arroyo Grande, CA*

SEWING WITH CONED THREAD: TWO TIPS

In order to use economical coned thread on a conventional sewing machine, I attached an eye screw near the top of an empty wooden thread spool, perpendicular to the spool's axis (if the screw has an opening, it should face up—see Fig. 109). I place the spool on the spindle of the machine with the eye to the back, set the cone of thread behind the machine, and thread through the eye screw, then through the rest of the machine as usual.

—*Nancy Camperud, Watsonville, CA*

When sewing with a large cone of thread, I place it in an empty coffee can on the floor and thread the machine as usual. Since the thread is below the machine, it unwinds easily.

—*Lois Carroll, Parma, OH*

THE NEEDLE-DOWN HABIT

Many newer sewing machines have a feature that allows you to specify whether the needle will stay down in the fabric or stop fully up whenever you lift your foot off the control. I ignored this feature except for turning corners until I finally discovered how much more control I had when I turned "needle-down" on for all my sewing, disengaging it only at the end of a seam. When you're topstitching or easing sleeves, or any time you're stopping mid-seam to adjust fab-

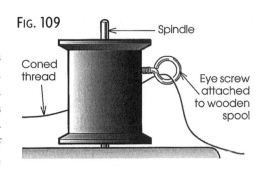

FIG. 109

Spindle

Coned thread

Eye screw attached to wooden spool

ric layers or check their position, having the needle down when you stop prevents slippage, even on the silkiest fabrics that presser feet alone can't keep secure. I'd retrain myself to stop needle down this way even if I didn't have the automatic feature. It's improved all my sewing.
—*Kathy Zachry, Springdale, AR*

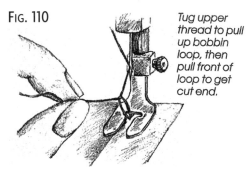

Tug upper thread to pull up bobbin loop, then pull front of loop to get cut end.

PULLING UP THE BOBBIN THREAD

If you need to pull up the bobbin thread end at the beginning of stitching, with fabric in the sewing machine, here's the correct way: Take one complete stitch, with the presser foot down; tug on the upper thread tail to bring up a loop of the bobbin thread, as shown in Fig. 110. Now pull the front or right side of the bobbin thread loop to bring up the cut end of the thread. If you pull on the back or left side of the loop, you'll reel thread off the bobbin instead.

TOPSTITCHING ENDS INVISIBLY

To secure a line of topstitching, tie your threads and weave the ends into the fabric instead of backstitching. Pull the top thread to the back and tie the threads. Leave thread tails long enough to thread into an embroidery needle.

Weave the needle in between the layers of fabric for ½ in. and out again on the back. Pull gently to cause some tension and snip the thread at the fabric line, which will cause the thread to disappear between the layers.
—*Mary Hardenbrook, Huntington Beach, CA*

WHY BACKSTITCH?

Since I discovered the technique of reducing my stitch length to 1mm or less to secure the stitching at the start and end of a seam instead of backstitching, I've abandoned backstitching entirely. Reducing the stitch length is no harder or slower. and I never have to tie off loose threads. It's also a great, bulk-free way to end the stitching at the point of a dart.
—*Phyllis Stillwell, El Cajon, CA*

FLATTENING THICK SEAMS

Sometimes thick details of a sewing project (e.g., the comer where two narrow hems meet.) are impossible to fit under the presser foot. Before stitching, I compress these areas with a pair of vise grips. Clamp the vise grips on the problem spot and turn the adjustment knob to flatten the area as much as possible. Be sure to protect your fashion fabric by wrapping the jaws of the vise grips with sturdy scrap fabric.
—*D. Self, Aurora, CO*

STITCHING AN ACCURATE EDGE

When topstitching near edges, the needle tends to roll off the fabric because there is an uneven surface under the presser foot. Place a piece of cardboard or fabric of the same thickness as the fabric edge under the low side of the presser foot. Leveling the surface will let you stitch with perfect control.

—*Elaine MacKay, Thamesford, Ontario, Canada*

GETTING A HANDLE ON SEWING DETAILS

I always had trouble edgestitching shirt collars on my zigzag machine. When I got to the point of the collar and turned the work to sew the long edge, the needle would push the point down into the slot in the throat plate or pull it up into the slot in the presser foot. It was also hard to guide the collar for neat stitching because there wasn't much fabric for my fingers or the feed dogs to grasp.

I solved this problem by slipping a piece of paper (from a small note pad) under the collar about 1 in. before reaching the point. I sew through the fabric and the paper, using the paper as a handle to help guide the stitching. The paper tears away easily after stitching. This works for all pointed construction details, such as cuffs, sashes, belts, and lapels.

—*D. Self, Aurora, CO*

TOPSTITCHING CLOSE TO CORNERS

I've found a good way to prevent the sewing machine from "eating" the fabric as you top-stitch close to the edges around corners. Thread a needle with a double strand, but don't knot it. Take one stitch through the very edge of the corner, as shown in Fig. 111. As you sew up to the corner and around it, hold the two ends of the thread so the corner won't be pulled down into the throat plate.

—*Mary A. Roehr, Memphis, TN*

BOBBIN THREADS FOR DOUBLE NEEDLES

To prevent making tucks you don't want when you're stitching with a double needle, use wooly nylon thread (usually sold for sergers) in the bobbin. Its slight stretch and extra thickness require loosening the bobbin tension, which I always do with the bobbin inside a small plastic bag so I don't have to worry about losing the tiny adjusting screw. You also have to wind the bobbin by hand to avoid stretching the thread before stitching, but the great-looking results justify the extra effort.

—*Carol Gee, Newtown, CT*

FIG. 111

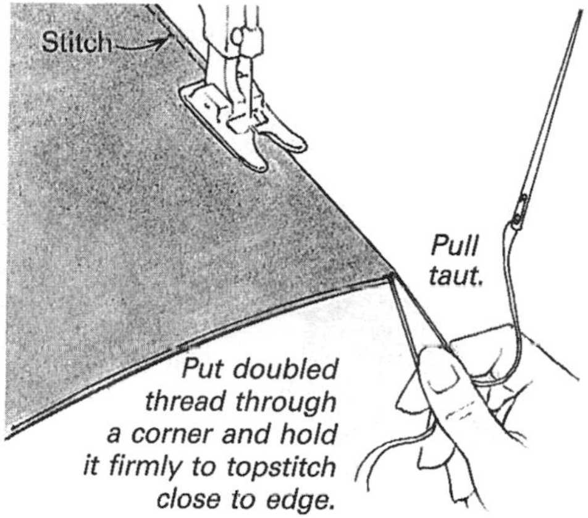

Stitch

Pull taut.

Put doubled thread through a corner and hold it firmly to topstitch close to edge.

FIG. 112

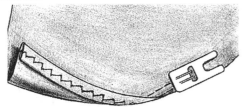

A twin needle and the regular foot makes a slightly stretchy topstitched hem for knits.

FIG. 113

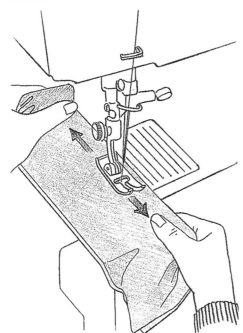

A STRETCHY STRAIGHT STITCH

You can produce a straight stitch with some built-in stretch for topstitching hems on garments made of knit fabric by using a twin needle and the regular sewing-machine foot, as shown in Fig. 112.

—*Ruth. J. Falls, Morehead City, NC*

TAUT SEWING

Taut sewing is a useful machine-sewing technique to keep fabric layers from shifting during sewing; use it for velvet as well as for slippery fabrics. Hold the fabric layers together behind the needle with two fingers and in front of the needle with your whole hand (Fig. 113), then pull in both directions with slight to medium pressure. This is what makes the fabric "taut." If you pull too tightly, the feed dogs won't be able to advance the fabric properly. Practice on scraps to get the tension right. Taut sewing flattens velvet's pile and helps it to feed more easily under the presser foot. In slippery fabrics, such as silky polyesters, it reduces puckering.

EASING

You can use the action of the feed dog to ease two fabric pieces of uneven length. The action of the feed dog tends to pull the bottom piece of fabric through more quickly than the top layer, which is apparent when you sew two equal-length pieces of fabric together and find that they don't match up at the end of the seam. You can use this tendency to your advantage when easing together two pieces of unequal length. This technique works especially well on shoulder seams, waistbands, and dropped-shoulder sleeves. With practice, you can even use the feed dog to ease a set-in sleeve into the armscye.

Pin the two layers of fabric at the ends and at the center, and place them under the foot with the longer piece on the bottom. For shorter lengths, it isn't necessary to pin; you can simply hold the center and the end firmly between each thumb and index finger. As you stitch, make sure the raw edges match, and let the feed dogs ease the longer bottom layer into the shorter top one.

MACHINE-EASED SLEEVE CAPS

My mother taught me a good way to ease in the cap of a set-in sleeve. It eliminates the puckers that are often associated with the use of machine gathering stitches.

Using a regular stitch length, start machine-stitching slowly from one notch in the sleeve along the seamline to the other notch. To ease the cap as you stitch, use the eraser end of a pencil in one hand and the fingertips of your other hand to push the fabric gently toward the back of the presser foot on both sides, as shown in Fig. 114. Start pushing about ½ to ¾ in. in front of the needle. Stop when the fabric is a little beyond the needle, reposition the pencil, push again, and repeat until you reach the other notch. Sometimes I stretch the fabric outward while pushing back, which eases even more. The result will be a sleeve with a nice cap and no puckers in the seam line.

If more or less ease is needed, simply push more or less as you stitch. You can also pull on the thread or clip it to adjust the gathers while inserting the sleeve in the armhole.
—*Janet Earnhardt, Utica, PA*

FIG. 114

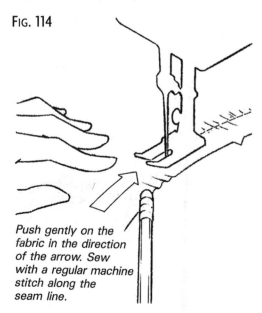

Push gently on the fabric in the direction of the arrow. Sew with a regular machine stitch along the seam line.

AN EASY WAY TO GATHER FABRIC

Lay a piece of heavy thread (buttonhole twist, crochet cotton) next to the seamline, on the seam-allowance side, and sew a narrow zigzag stitch over it. (Be careful not to catch the thread in the stitching.) Then pull the heavy thread to form gathers. The zigzag stitches will make a channel, so you can pull the heavy thread through easily, without tugging or breaking threads.

This method works especially well for gathering long ruffled curtains, but is just as useful for short gathers, such as on sleeve caps. Simply keep your zigzag stitches within the seam allowance, and no stitches will show when the garment is put together.
—*Corinne Elworth, Orrtanna, PA*

EASY GATHERED PLEATS

Cartridge pleating is difficult to do evenly and frustrating if your thread breaks before you finish the gathers. To avoid this difficulty and speed the process, I stitch over a thread. Press under the seam allowance or facing at the top edge. Set your sewing machine to its widest blind-hem stitch. Place a length of button-and-carpet thread where you want to start your first row of pleating, and blindstitch over the thread. Do a second row exactly like the first, keeping

FIG. 115

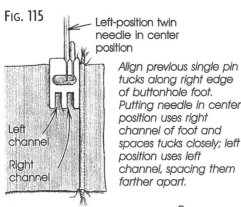

Left-position twin needle in center position

Align previous single pin tucks along right edge of buttonhole foot. Putting needle in center position uses right channel of foot and spaces tucks closely; left position uses left channel, spacing them farther apart.

Left channel

Right channel

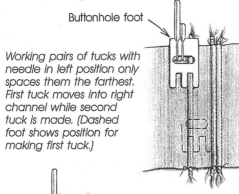

Buttonhole foot

Working pairs of tucks with needle in left position only spaces them the farthest. First tuck moves into right channel while second tuck is made. (Dashed foot shows position for making first tuck.)

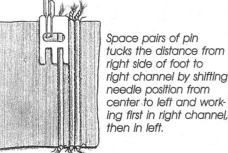

Space pairs of pin tucks the distance from right side of foot to right channel by shifting needle position from center to left and working first in right channel, then in left.

the rows evenly spaced and the blindstitches matched one below the other, and pull both threads evenly.

—*Pamela Tallman, Huntington Beach, CA*

PLEATER ALTERNATIVE

If you don't own a pleater and don't want to pay someone to pleat for you, try this. Thread your sewing machine with a triple needle. Using the pin-tucking foot, stitch as many rows as you need. With these lines as your guide, you can make very pretty hand or machine smocking.

—*Ellen J. Riggan, Gloucester, VA*

PIN-TUCKING WITH A BUTTONHOLE FOOT

If you can't get a pin-tuck foot for your sewing machine or wouldn't use it enough to justify the cost, you can use the buttonhole foot of your zigzag machine. Its limitations are that there is only one channel size, and no more than two tucks can be made side by side. You'll also need a 2mm left-position twin needle and a machine with a front- or top-loaded bobbin and the ability to shift the needle position left and right (see Fig. 115). The narrow channels of the foot provide enough stability, so a fabric stabilizer isn't needed for most fabrics.

Turn the flywheel by hand to lower the needle until it just pierces the fabric. If you're using a cord, make sure it's between the two needles and moves freely. Grasp the three sewing threads firmly while taking the first two to three stitches. Once you've started, you can concentrate on guiding the work. As I complete each tuck, I pull the cord through until the excess at the top is eliminated before I cut the work from the machine.

To use the foot as a guide for spacing single tucks, set the needle position at whichever channel gives the desired distance. The center needle position makes use of the right channel, which spaces the tucks rather close. The left needle position uses the left channel and spaces them a little farther apart.

For pairs of tucks, set the needle to the left, sew the first tuck, move the tuck into the right channel, and sew the second tuck (middle drawing at left). You can continue this way, spacing the pairs of tucks the distance from the right edge of the foot to the left channel. Or you can space them a little closer by shifting the needle between center and left positions and working first in the right channel and then in the left (bottom drawing at left). You can also space the tucks without regard to the presser-foot width. As with a special pin-tuck foot, you can also do cord quilting.

—*Elizabeth Lee Richter, Huntington, CT*

MACHINE HEMMING WITH LACE

Here's an almost magical, all-machine finishing technique for attaching lace edging to very fine fabrics such as cotton batiste and silk while creating a tiny rolled and whipped hem. It's perfect for finishing fine lingerie and linings. Position the lace edging face down on the right side of your fabric, about ⅛ in. from the raw edge. With the needle centered and set to zigzag, adjust the stitch width so that the needle catches the lace heading on the left and clears the fabric on the right, as shown in Fig. 116. Set your stitch

FIG. 116

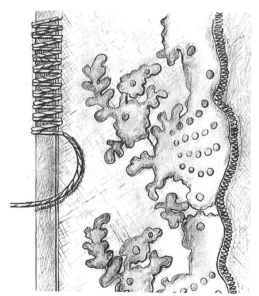

length to a near satin stitch, then increase the needle-thread tension. Here are my setttings, which you may have to tweak: Width: 3½ to 4mm; length: 20 sts./in.; tension: 7½ to 8. Starting at the left, insert the needle into the lace heading, lower the presser foot, and begin stitching slowly and evenly. The tension on the needle thread will roll the fabric up and over, and the zigzag will enclose the raw edge. Press the lace and fabric open. If your lace is gathered, it works best to straight-stitch the lace down first, then zigzag over the straight stitching and off the edge as described.
—*Gail Manning, Don Mills, Ontario, Canada*

EDGING LINGERIE

For an attractive scallop-edge finish on lingerie or lightweight garments, I use the blind stitch on my machine. First, finish the edge by serging, or turn the raw edge under ¼ in.; then fold on the seam allowance and press. Do a test strip by setting the stitch width to the widest setting (4) and the stitch length in the middle (2). With the wrong side up, put the fabric under the presser foot with the edge to the left and the garment to the right of the needle. Feed the fabric through so that when the occasional zigzag stitch bites, it grabs just outside the finished edge. It is this zigzag stitch that forms the scalloped edge.
—*Elizabeth Rydman, Santa Fe, NM*

APPLY LACE WITH BLIND STITCH

Here's an attractive and virtually invisible lace application that works equally well whether the lace will lie flat on the completed garment or will be an edge finish. If flat, place the lace on or adjacent to the placement line, wrong side up and pointing in the opposite direction to its finished position. With the blind-hem setting on your machine, and with thread that matches the lace, stitch on the placement line next to the lace edge, just catching it with the swing stitch, as shown in Fig. 117. I've found that a stitch length of 3mm and a width of 1mm work

well, but experiment to find a good setting for your machine. Gently turn the lace down over the line of stitching (it pivots inside the tiny swing stitch), and press. For an edge finish, begin by placing the lace wrong side up with the lace band just above the hemline. Since this lace will be on the edge of the garment and may take more of a beating, use a shorter stitch length when you attach it. Press the lace down, turning the hem at the same time. Finish the hem however you desire.

—*Andrea Moore, Spokane, WA*

FIG. 117

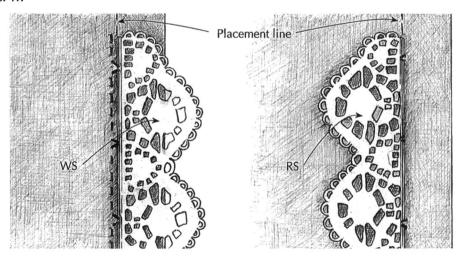

Placement line

WS

RS

ATTACHING TRIMS BY MACHINE

Here's another use for the blind hemstitch found on most modern sewing machines. I was adding tiny, prestrung costume-jewelry pearls to a garment. I sewed the string on by blind hemming next to it so the straight stitches were alongside the string, and the sideways stitches caught it. When I used my adjustable zipper foot to get up close, it worked like a charm. After experimenting, I developed several ways to do it.

One way is to fold the material where you want the trim and then to run the fold under the zipper foot so the sideways part of the blind hemstitch falls off the edge. Hold the trim close to the fold, and it will be caught by the stitch.

This creates a tuck where the fold is and works on straight lines only. The fold can be an edge or can occur in the middle of the fabric, but don't forget to allow for the material taken up by the tuck.

When you want the trim right on a curved edge, face the curve and turn the garment right side out. Then run the curved edge and trim under the foot, as described above.

In both cases, I usually use a thread that matches the fabric so it won't be seen, and I make the stitch width as narrow as possible. If you want to use a thread that matches the trim, not the fabric, or don't want the little tuck, leave the fabric flat as you stitch, and fold it at the trim later. The stitches will be on the inside of the fold only. This will also work on faced edges. Stitch the trim onto the seamline of the garment piece, with the stitches in the seam allowance, before attaching the facing, as shown in Fig. 118.
—Doris Gray, Blythewood, SC

LENGTH GUIDE FOR BUTTONHOLES

To measure my buttonholes accurately when I'm using the automatic buttonholer on my zigzag machine, I use a strip of see-through graph paper, found in architectural or office-supply stores. Place the button on the grid and mark the number of squares required for the buttonhole. After marking the buttonholes on the fabric, lay the graph-paper template over the buttonhole line. Sew each buttonhole the length of the template. Simply tear away the paper when finished.
—Pam Hobson, Anacortes WA

EVEN BUTTONHOLES

Since my machine doesn't have a special attachment for buttonholes, I've developed my own method for making uniform, straight ones. I use a peel-off mailing label, cutting out a rectangle the length and width of the buttonhole from the center. I stick it on the garment where I need the buttonhole, and stitch inside the rectangle. This template can be moved and reused several times before it loses its adhesive. Then it's a simple matter to make another.
—Terry Grant, Ashland, OR

MAKING BUTTONHOLES

Here's a way to make buttonholes come out the right length. Mark the beginning of the buttonhole with a basting line. Line up the sewing-machine needle with that point, and lower the presser foot. Then mark the position of the back of the foot by placing a pin in the fabric a little

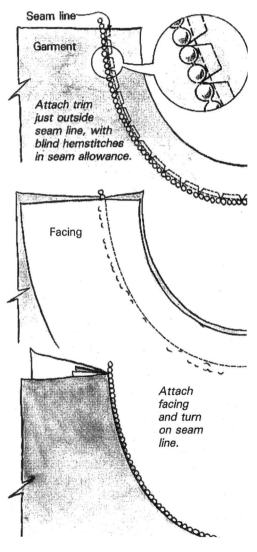

FIG. 118

Seam line

Garment

Attach trim just outside seam line, with blind hemstitches in seam allowance.

Facing

Attach facing and turn on seam line.

FIG. 119

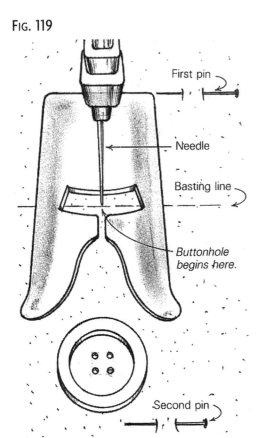

First pin

Needle

Basting line

Buttonhole begins here.

Second pin

off to one side, as shown in Fig. 119. Now put the button in front of the foot, and put a second pin in front of the button, allowing a little space for reinforcing the ends of the buttonhole, and for ease.

Take the button away and stitch one side of the buttonhole. When the front of the foot reaches the second pin, reinforce the end of the buttonhole. Then stitch the other side of the buttonhole, stopping when the back of the foot has returned to the first pin. Reinforce the end, and your buttonhole should be perfect.
—*Ruth S. Galpin, Southport, CT*

EASY BUTTONHOLE MARKERS
To help make sure all my machine-made buttonholes come out the same size, I use a template made from a Post-it Note stick-on. First draw a line on the note parallel to the sticky edge the distance you want your buttonholes from the edge of the buttonhole band. This marks your buttonhole line when you stick the template on the fold of the fabric, as in Fig. 120. Then cut two lines on the adhesive edge of the note the same distance apart as the length of your buttonhole and deeper than the buttonhole placement line. Fold back the middle section, stick the note onto the garment at the

mark for the first buttonhole, and stitch between the unfolded flaps of the note. Yellow notes work well on most colors of fabric, but you can get other colors if you need them.
—*Mimi Anderson, Tacoma, WA*

FIG. 120

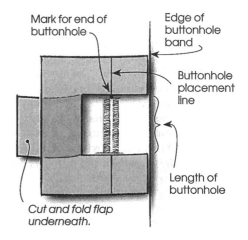

Mark for end of buttonhole

Edge of buttonhole band

Buttonhole placement line

Length of buttonhole

Cut and fold flap underneath.

MACHINE SEWING BUTTONS
I hate sewing on buttons by hand, but when I sewed on nonshank buttons by machine, they slipped around under the presser foot and ended up sewn too tightly, which puckered the buttonhole side of a garment. Now I sew on buttons with the aid of a thin plastic card with a slot cut in one edge (I cut expired credit cards and thinner check-cashing ID cards, which work well for

finer fabrics). I put a small dot of Velcro glue (available at notions counters where Velcro is sold) at the end of the slot (Fig. 121) and press the button down, centering the button stitching holes over the slot. The card holds the button steady under the presser foot and provides just enough space between the button and fabric for buttoning ease. I set the machine for the appropriate zigzag width, drop the feed dog, and sew. Any glue residue on the card or the back of the button is easy to rub off.

—*Barbara McGraw, Lancaster, PA*

FIG. 121

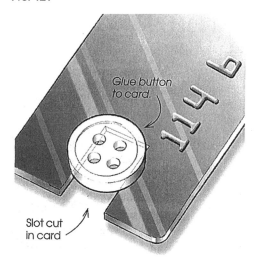

Glue button to card.

Slot cut in card

CORDED BUTTONHOLES

To make corded buttonholes on the sewing machine, stitch a regular buttonhole over a loop of heavy thread, embroidery floss, or several strands of the buttonhole thread. The zigzag stitches should cover, but not catch, the thread so it can be pulled up tightly to the bar tack at the loop end after stitching, as in Fig. 122. Thread the loose cord ends on a needle, pull to the wrong side or between the fabric layers, and tie to secure. Check your machine manual to see if your buttonhole foot has a prong or grooves to hold the cord in place as you stitch.

BASTING TAPE HOLDS BUTTONS

The automatic button-sewing feature on my sewing machine doesn't hold buttons firmly. After breaking a few buttons and bending too many needles, I devised the following system to keep the buttons in place: Place a piece of double-faced basting tape under one side of the button to hold it in place while it is being sewn down. Be sure to place the tape out of the way of the sewing holes. Remove the tape when the button is sewn.

—*Edna Isaac, Tulsa, OK*

FIG. 122

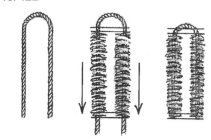

RIPPING A SEAM

To rip a seam means to cut and remove the stitching. The most common tool sewers use to rip is either a small pair of scissors or a seam ripper (a handle with a C-shaped blade mounted on the end—see Fig. 123A). Expert alterationist Melissa Ingling-Leath avoids seam rippers, however, because she's found that they can easily cut the fabric. Instead, she suggests ripping with a pair of 4-in. embroidery scissors, which give her more control over the process.

For her basic technique, Ingling-Leath suggests working from the wrong side to minimize the possibility of snagging the face of the garment and to reduce the number of loose threads that remain on the right side after ripping. Separating the layers of the seam, clip several stitches, then pull the seam apart as far as you

can without forcing it and clip a few more stitches, as shown in Fig. 123B. (Forcing the seam open may result in holes, especially on a soft or delicate fabric.) Repeat the process until the required ripping is complete.

Ingling-Leath uses another ripping technique that's quicker but can be used only on firm fabrics, such as gabardine. Holding the scissors open, slip the blade inside the layers and glide it along the seam, ripping the stitches (Fig. 123C). This method takes practice: You need to keep some tension on the fabric to cut the stitches, but with too much tension you may accidentally slice through the fabric.

Another method leaves no bits of cut thread on the fabric. With a straight pin or seam ripper, pick out about 1 to 1½ in. of stitches, without cutting the thread. Grab the thread end, pull (which gathers the seam), and break the thread as close as possible to the seam. On the other side of the fabric, you'll find a loose end of thread. Pick it free with your fingernail, then grab it, pull, and break. Repeat the process on alternate sides of the fabric until the seam is ripped.

The ripped-out seam always looks best with all the clipped stitches removed. So if you use a ripping technique that leaves cut threads, you can pat along the seamline with a strip or loop of packing tape, which will remove some of the thread ends. But, alas, the only way to get rid of every last thread is to pick them off bit by bit, by hand. And that's the slow part of ripping a seam.

FIG. 123A

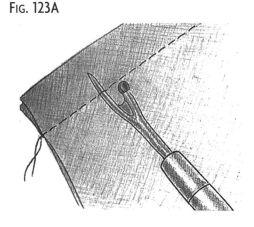

FIG. 123B

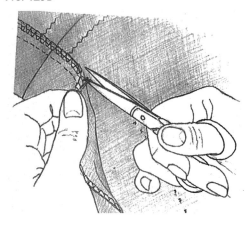

FIG. 123C

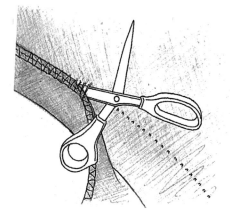

RIPPING LOCKSTITCH

I never use a seam ripper for removing lock-stitch, partly from fear of cutting the fabric, but more from loathing of picking the tiny thread bits. I use an X-Acto knife and my presser foot as a third hand.

Pull the stitching apart as far as possible without risking tearing, and maintain continued light pressure with your left hand. With the tip of the X-Acto knife, cut only the lowest stitch you can see (Fig. 124). The stitches above it will release, and those below will spread.

As each section opens, the position of the work shifts suddenly, so practice on a scrap to learn to anticipate it and to develop the right reflex with your knife hand so you won't cut the fabric. With practice, good eyesight, good light, and good luck with the original thread tension, you'll be able to leave all the cut threads on one side, with only one long one on the other side. The cut threads will be fewer and longer than those left by a conventional seam ripper, and they'll be far easier to pick.
—*Marianne Kantor, Bondville, VT*

SEAM-HOLE REPAIR

When you remove a hem or rip apart a seam, lots of little holes remain. To remove them, dampen a cloth with white vinegar, spread it flat under the material, and press.
—*Suzen Wiener, Spring Hill, FL*

SAFER SEAM RIPPING

If you have to rip apart an old garment in order to make a pattern, first spray the seam allowances with spray starch and iron them. This will prevent the fabric from losing its shape when you pull the seams apart.
—*Marilyn A. Jensen, Fremont, CA*

SEAM RIPPER

I find it a lot easier to rip seams with a small pair of needle-nose pliers than with any other tool I've used. Wrap the tips of the pliers with masking tape to improve the grip. Use your seam ripper to break the seam at about 1-in. intervals, and pick one or two stitches out at each break (Fig. 125). Grab the broken thread with the pliers, and pull straight out, not toward yourself, in the direction of the seam.
—*Susan Herrmann, Damascus, OH*

RIPPING OUT MACHINE-MADE SATIN STITCH

Here's an easy way to rip out the densely packed stitches you get with computer embroidery and monogramming, buttonholes, or any kind of satin stitch: Shave off the bobbin-side threads with a few strokes of a disposable razor. As long as the fabric stays taut while you shave, you'll be in no danger of cutting the fabric.
—*Princesa Alexander, Henrietta, TX*

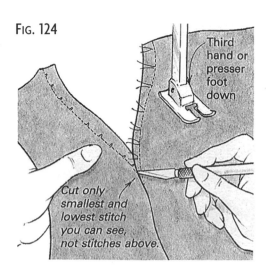

FIG. 124

Third hand or presser foot down

Cut only smallest and lowest stitch you can see, not stitches above.

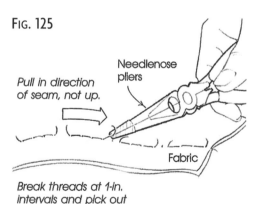

FIG. 125

Pull in direction of seam, not up.

Needlenose pliers

Fabric

Break threads at 1-in. intervals and pick out two stitches.

Chapter 8

❖

FABRICS

SHEER AND SLIPPERY FABRICS

Working with soft, slippery, sheer fabrics such as chiffons or georgettes is not difficult if you know a few tricks, suggests sewing instructor Sandra Betzina. To prevent sheer fabrics from slipping on the cutting table, cover the table with tissue paper at least as long and half as wide as your fabric. To avoid snagging the fabric with blunt or burred pins, use new glass-head silk pins, which are thin and have sharp points that easily pierce fine fabrics. Also, be sure your hands and nails are smooth before you handle a sheer.

Fold the fabric lengthwise and pin the double thickness to the tissue paper along the selvages and crosswise edges to keep the grain straight. Pin the pattern pieces to the fabric and tissue paper, then use sharp scissors such as Gingher serrated shears to cut through the fabric and paper. The paper stabilizes the fabric and helps you cut accurately shaped pattern pieces.

For machine-sewing sheers, use a fine sewing-machine needle with a sharp (not a universal) point, such as a Schmetz 70/10 HJ needle. For this fabric and needle, use a fine 60-weight, all-cotton embroidery thread or lingerie thread, which produces a flatter, less noticeable seam than heavier thread.

Unlike seam allowances in opaque fabrics, seams in sheers will show, so you'll want to finish them neatly. Also, seams in sheers tend to ravel, pucker, and split unless carefully sewn.

For a neat, short seam on a blouse or shirt, use a narrow French seam. To make this seam, assuming the pattern has a ⅝-in. seam allowance, first place the wrong sides of the fabric together and sew a ⅜-in. seam. Trim the seam allowance to ⅛ in., then enclose the seam by placing right sides of the fabric together, pressing, and sewing a ¼-in. seam (Fig. 126A).

Sewing a French seam with straight stitching may cause long vertical seams on pants and skirts to draw up. To prevent puckering in long seams, you can use one of the following two alternatives: Sew a French seam as described, but use a narrow zigzag (.5mm) for both lines of stitching to give the seam elasticity, or combine a line of zigzag with one of serging. To make the zigzagged/serged seam, first sew the seam on a conventional sewing machine using a medium stitch length and a narrow (.5mm) zigzag. Next move to the serger, lengthen the distance between stitches to reduce the amount of thread in the seam, and serge the seam allowances together just next to the zigzag stitching.

For a fast, professional-looking hem for sheers, use a machine-rolled hem. To make this hem, you'll need a rolled-hem foot (Fig. 126B). First machine-stitch ¼ in. from the edge of the fabric and trim close to the stitching. Then, to start the hem, roll the edge of the fabric by hand, place it under the foot, and sew a couple of stitches on top of the rolled edge. Stop with

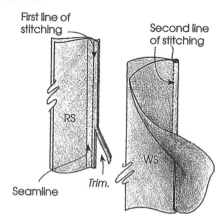

FIG. 126A

First line of stitching

Second line of stitching

RS

WS

Seamline

Trim.

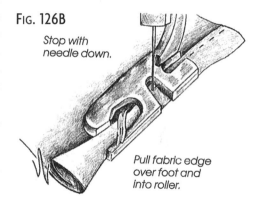

FIG. 126B

Stop with needle down.

Pull fabric edge over foot and into roller.

the needle in the fabric and pull the fabric edge over the foot and into the roller. Without stretching the fabric, gently pull it to the left as you stitch to keep a consistent amount of fabric rolled into the hem.

INTERFACING SHEER FABRICS

When using sewn-in interfacing on sheer fabrics, baste it to the top collar piece rather than the undercollar. The interfacing serves as a lining, hiding the seam allowance so it doesn't show through.
—*Edith Frankel, Hannawa Falls, NY*

DEFENDING AGAINST SEAM SLIPPAGE

Rayons and other slippery, loose fabrics that tend to slip or shred at the seamline can be supported without significant bulk with ½-in.-wide bias bands of fusible nylon tricot. Apply the bands about ⅜ in. in from each cutting line before sewing so the seamline (assuming ⅝-in. seam allowances) is centered under the bands. Alternative interfacings include a combination of fusible web and a seam binding such as Seams Great, or a lightweight fusible such as Easy Knit or Sew Sheer.
—*Lauren Hunt, East Lansing, MI*

PERFECTLY MATCHED THREAD AND FABRIC

To get perfectly matched threads for hems and topstitching when sewing silks, unravel a few yards of weft from a torn straight edge and wind it onto an empty spool. Since raw silk is too nubby and silk taffetas and china silks tend to be fragile, some experimentation is necessary.
—*Sandra A. Tebbs, Tremonton, UT*

PINNING SILK

People usually think of silk as a delicate fabric because of the special care it requires. But silk fiber is as strong as steel. And if you've ever worked with tightly woven silks, such as china or satin silk, then you know that it's sometimes nearly impossible to pierce the fabric with the point of a pin, regardless of the quality of the pin used. And you never want to force the issue because silk will run. My trick for pinning such fabrics works like a charm. It's "acupuncture"! As you bring the point of the pin to the fabric, spin the pin between your fingers. It will slide in with little or no resistance.
—*Victoria Valdes-Dapena-Hiltebeitel, Collegeville, PA*

VELVET

Velvet is a luxury fabric that is often reserved for special-occasion fashions. From time to time, however, it emerges as an everyday fabric. Distinguished by its luster and deep, rich pile, velvet comes in different fiber contents. Cotton and cotton-blend velvets are sometimes washable, and thus a good choice for children's clothes. More expensive silk and silk/rayon velvets have a soft, sensuous drape and are suitable for styles with gathers and soft pleats. The most popular and readily available velvets are all-rayon, rayon/acetate, and rayon/acetate/nylon blends. These velvets are often used for jackets, vests, and skirts.

As a pile fabric, velvet needs to be cut using a "with nap" layout, where all the pieces are laid out with the nap in the same direction. This usually requires additional fabric, so it's a good idea to do a trial layout with your pattern pieces to see how many yards you'll need. By stroking velvet, you can feel the nap's direction. In the downward direction, the nap feels softer and smoother. The two directions also show different colorations. If you cut your garment with the nap running downward, the velvet will take on a duller, frosted coloration. When the nap runs upward, the color looks richer and darker.

Most sewers decide to cut velvet using the upward nap direction for a more luxurious color. However, for longer durability and less crushing of the pile in elbows and seat, some sewers select the downward direction.

After you've decided on the nap direction for your garment, it's a good idea to draw a large arrow on each pattern piece, indicating the intended layout. If your pattern includes a collar, don't forget to check how it will lie on the body to determine the nap direction (see Fig. 127).

MACHINE BASTING VELVETS

You can eliminate uneven seams in velvets, corduroys, and other napped and tricky fabrics right on your sewing machine by tacking both ends of the seam, exactly on the seamline, with three or four regular-length straight stitches. Next find the center of the seam, and tack again. Continue dividing the seam sections in half and tacking with a few stitches until the seam has been secured every few inches. If your basting stitches are accurately placed on the seamline, you don't even have to remove them. Just stitch right over them for a flawless seam.
—Andrea Moore, Spokane, WA

PINNING WITH TAPE

I use double-sided sticky tape when sewing leather, velvet, or silk. It holds two layers together without allowing shifting, and it can be removed easily after a seam has been stitched.
—Marli Popple, Armadale, Victoria, Australia

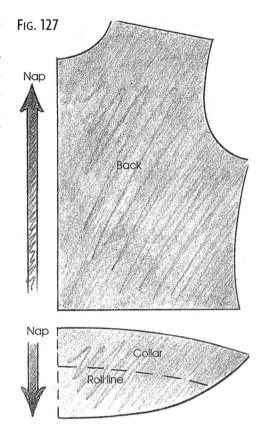

FIG. 127

Nap

Back

Nap

Collar

Roll line

REMOVING CREASES FROM VELVET

Remodeling vintage garments made of velvet requires some experimentation to remove the lines left by hem edges, seams, and topstitching. Here are some techniques that have worked for me. Wet the crease with vinegar to soften the fibers and help them unkink. Gently raise the pile with a stiff toothbrush. Velvet can be steamed by pressing very lightly on the back with a warm iron (hot iron if the fiber content allows). A blow dryer can be used on the right side to encourage the pile to lift. Steaming the surface of the fabric can be done by holding the iron over it no closer than 1 in. A scrap of cotton velvet can be used as a press cloth; press lightly, right sides together.
—*Susan Herrmann, Damascus, OH*

LEATHER AND SUEDE

Leather and suede are sold by the skin or hide and priced by the square foot. Garment-weight leather is the lightest weight leather available, at about 1 to 1½ oz. per square foot. When estimating your needs, add 10 to 15 percent to allow for imperfections in the skin. Mail-order catalogs generally include the weight per square foot and the square footage per skin.

If you need to iron leather or suede to remove wrinkles or press seam allowances open, use a medium-hot, dry iron. Test on a piece of scrap first, since an iron that is too hot will crackle and shrink leather and suede. Working over a layer of brown paper or a lightweight press cloth, press with little movement of the iron to prevent stretching.

INVISIBLE PINNING FOR LEATHER AND SUEDE

When stitching suede, Ultrasuede, or leather, I normally use paper clips to hold garment pieces together as I stitch them. When I match two crossing seamlines exactly, however, I use a common pin. By inserting the pin between the threads of the already completed seams (see Fig. 128), not only can I align the seams accurately, but I also avoid marring the leather.
—*Judith Brandau, Butler, PA*

FIG. 128

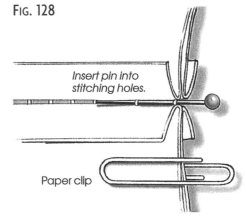

Insert pin into stitching holes.

Paper clip

BASTING LEATHER OR VINYL

Basting is difficult and pinning is impossible when you're working with leather or vinyl. My solution is to use staples in the seam allowance. You can use almost any stapler, but the pliers type is handier than the desk-top version. After you've done the stitching, you can easily remove the staples with a small pair of needle-nosed pliers or a staple remover.

—Betty Sager, Spring Valley, CA

NEEDLES FOR LEATHER

To sew leather and fur by hand or machine, you'll need special needles, which are available at local sewing stores. Called *glover's needles* for hand sewing and *leather needles* for the machine, these needles, shown in Fig. 129, have a wedge-shaped point that cuts easily into leather and fur and reduces skipped stitches.

SEWING WITH ULTRASUEDE AND FACILE

Since I do a lot of sewing with Ultrasuede and Facile, I have discovered several handy techniques. Skipped stitches can be prevented on Ultrasuede if you use the Schmetz Stretch 75/11 needle (steel-blue color). I cut binding trim on the crosswise rather than the bias grain, and to make sure my strips are even, I use masking tape on the wrong side as a guide. Sometimes I combine two or more tape widths for odd sizes. It's easier if you cut only one section of a double-faced Ultrasuede belt accurately. You can fuse it to a slightly larger piece of Ultrasuede, topstitch, and then trim off the excess.

I like to use Facile for suits that combine a soft, drapey skirt with a more tailored jacket. I underline the major jacket pieces by fusing Easy-Knit right to them to provide a little more body. Be sure to preshrink the Easy-Knit in warm water, and dry it flat or hung. Voila! Flow and fit with the same fabric.

—Alida Macor, Martinsville, NJ

MUSLIN

Muslin is a soft, plain-woven cotton fabric that is relatively inexpensive, especially in its unbleached form. For this reason it is often used to interface lightweight garments, line or underline garments, and test patterns for style and fit.

LINEN

Woven linen fabrics have been used for making clothing for thousands of years. According to Claire Shaeffer's *Fabric Sewing Guide* (Radnor, PA: Chilton, 1989), the fiber for linen comes from the stem of the flax plant, and it weaves into a fabric that dyes well and is easy to sew and press. Although it tends to wrinkle easily, linen sheds surface dirt and resists staining.

FIG. 129

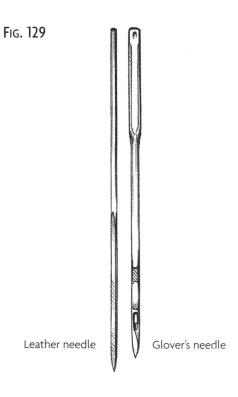

Leather needle   Glover's needle

When shopping for a linen fabric, it's important to recognize quality. High-quality linen fabric feels cool, smooth, and supple, while inexpensive fabrics are stiffer, coarser, and often have heavy sizing (a surface finish that temporarily gives the fabric more body). You can judge the quality of a linen fabric by examining the weave and yarn: The finer the yarns and the more threads per inch, the better the fabric.

CRYSTAL PLEATS

The process called "primitive pleating" lets you achieve an almost Fortuny-type look at home. A costume designer for theatre and opera passed it on to me when she heard of my love for crys-tal pleats. Start with 1½ to 2 times the amount of fabric the pattern calls for, depending on your pleats and how "floaty" you want your garment to be. Sew two rows of gathering stitches on both cut edges (Fig. 130). Pull the gathering threads up tight; then wet the fabric thoroughly. With a friend holding the other end, twist the fabric tightly until it knots up on itself. You can air-dry the fabric, but the pleats set more permanently if you dry it in the microwave on a low to medium-low setting. You know the setting is too hot if the fabric melts, so try a test swatch first. This method of pleating works best on polyester. The pleaks won't stay in a silk-satin charmeuse if you sit on them or get them wet.
—*Christina T. Paul, Lynnwood, WA*

FIG. 130

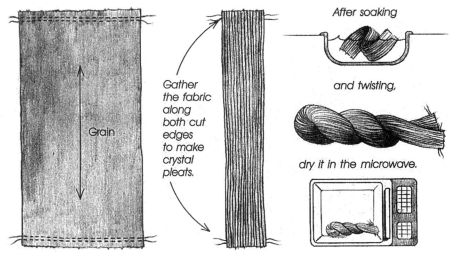

Grain

Gather the fabric along both cut edges to make crystal pleats.

After soaking

and twisting,

dry it in the microwave.

FABRICS FOR HEIRLOOM SEWING

Fabrics used in heirloom sewing include fine-quality, natural-fiber fabrics, most of which are semi-transparent. *Cotton or silk batiste* is a fine, semisoft, lightweight, plain-weave fabric that varies in sheerness. The finest-quality batiste is imported from Switzerland. *Organdy* is a sheer, permanently crisp cotton fabric woven with tightly twisted yarns. *Dotted Swiss* is a crisp, sheer cotton fabric with woven or flocked dots at regular intervals. *Handkerchief linen* is a lightweight, crisp fabric that ravels easily. *Silk organza* is a lightweight, sheer, plain-weave fabric, less crisp than organdy. *Silk chiffon* is a soft, sheer, slippery fabric woven from highly twisted yarns in a plain weave.

MARKING INFORMATION

I mark the selvage of newly purchased yardage with a washable marker, noting fiber content and number of yards. This way, even if I don't have a project in mind, I can store the fabric confident I won't forget this information.
—*Sara Tayloe, Arvada, CO*

NONRAVEL PRESHRINK

Before preshrinking a piece of fabric, try serging the raw edges in order to prevent raveling.
—*Pamela Smith, Dover-Foxcroft, ME*

TESTING FOR COLOR FASTNESS

Even though I always run my quilt fabrics through a wash cycle once before using them, I am never absolutely sure whether dark or red-toned fabrics will bleed color later. To test them further, I stitch a scrap of dark and light fabric together. I place the stitched swatch in a white china bowl full of hot water, and microwave it on high so the water boils. In a matter of minutes, I can tell if the fabric will bleed by looking at the color of the water. I can also check for any fabric shrinkage.
—*Solange Hawkins, Marietta, GA*

TESTING "DRY CLEAN" FABRIC FOR WASHABILITY

Cut a swatch in half and measure each piece. Put one piece in a bowl of cold, soapy water for three minutes. Rinse it in cold water, remove excess moisture with a towel, and let it dry, or press it dry if it's silk. Compare it with the unwashed half. Also test for water spotting by sprinkling some water on the swatch and letting it dry. To check the darker colors of prints for bleeding, fold a damp swatch in half and let it dry. If you plan to machine-wash, pin the measured swatch to a piece of stable fabric, and use the gentle cycle.
—*Susan Herrmann, Damascus, OH*

Keeping track of the right side

The next time you need to mark the right side of your garment pieces, place a tiny safety pin in the seam allowance on the right side of each piece as soon as you cut it. The pin won't rub off like chalk or leave a gummy residue the way tape would.

—Zulema Anté, Houston, TX

The right side of knits

A quick way to distinguish the right side of tricot or jersey knit is to stretch gently across the grain near a crosswise edge. The fabric will "roll" toward the right side.

—Janet Menec, Winnipeg, Manitoba, Canada

Cutting fabric ribbing

To make children's clothing, using ribbing for cuffs, waistbands, and neckbands, I used to waste time fiddling with the large chunks of ribbing fabric. Now I use a rotary cutter, yardstick, and grid mat to cut several strips at once in standard widths for cuffs and neckbands. I keep the strips in a basket, and just cut off the length I need.

—Charlene Pierce, Marshall, Saskatchewan, Canada

Fabric stiffener

Cotton-lace netting and other sheers straight from the bolt are never stiff enough to hold their shape. A concoction that stiffens even the limpest fabric is a mixture made from bits and pieces of water-soluble stabilizer. I dissolve a sandwich bag full of scraps with water until I get a thick, pudding-like mixture. (Proportions that work with Sulky Solvy are 1 yd. of soluble to ⅔ cup water.) My sandwich bag full was enough to coat a 35- by 25-in. piece of netting. When the fabric is thoroughly soaked, gently squeeze out the excess moisture, safety-pin the fabric to a wire hanger, and hang it outside to dry. Check on the fabric often and straighten any wrinkles.

—AnnMarie Wilson, Garland, TX

Serge with water-soluble stabilizer

Whenever I need to stabilize a silky fabric or prevent fabric from stretching while serging on bias edges, I use Solvy, a water-soluble stabilizer. Cut a 1-in.-wide strip of stabilizer a little longer than you need to complete the seam. Place the stabilizer under the serger foot with the end of the strip butted up to the cutting blade. Start stitching onto the stabilizer, allowing the blade to trim ¼ in. Now place the fabric on top of the stabilizer and under the serger foot and continue to stitch through the fabric and stabilizer. Trim

excess stabilizer from the reverse of your fabric; the remainder will disappear with the first wash.
—*Linda Lee Vivian, Lennon, MI*

MORE BODY FOR LACE

To give lace motifs the extra body they need for lingerie trim or beading application when sewing lingerie, try laminating two exact copies of the lace pattern together with fusible web. The webbing disappears after the fusing process, does not change the appearance of the lace, and leaves the lace firm enough to appliqué anywhere on the garment.
—*Andrea Moore, Spokane, WA*

SEWING FOAM-BACKED FABRIC

When sewing fabric that has a foam rubber backing, backing side up, try placing a piece of plastic wrap between the sewing-machine presser foot and the fabric. The fabric will move through the machine much more easily.
—*Susan L. Wiener, Spring Hill, FL*

INSTANT SPOT DEODORIZER

In our theatrical costume shop we must sometimes make emergency alterations or press musty or perspiration-soaked garments that we can't wash or dry-clean first. We've found that the odors can be removed with vodka. Spray full-strength vodka lightly on the garment immediately before pressing. The vodka evaporates odors away and leaves no smell.
—*Joan Morris, Hartford, VT*

BLOODSTAIN REMOVER

After a mishap with my new silk blouse at the blood drive, a nurse applied 20-volume hydrogen peroxide (used for bleaching hair) to the spots with a cotton swab. The spots bubbled, disappeared, and dried without a trace. I've since found that dried stains can be treated this way, but may take more than one application. Test the fabric first in an inconspicuous place, and wash thoroughly after treatment to remove any peroxide.
—*Carole Fisher, Framingham, MA*

BLOT AWAY BLOODSTAINS

A safe, foolproof method for removing needle-prick bloodstains from a garment-in-progress without damage is to use your own saliva. Wet a small piece of balled white thread or muslin with saliva, gently saturate the stain, and blot the area.
—*Elizabeth Stommel, Falmouth, MA*

Chapter 9

NOTIONS

EASY COVERED BUTTONS

Here's an improvement on the instructions that come with covered-button sets. It eliminates struggling to tuck the material around the pointed teeth of the metal button form.

Cut out circles of material to the size specified by the button manufacturer. Hand-sew a line of stitches that are slightly longer than normal length around the circumference of the circle, about $\frac{1}{16}$ to $\frac{1}{8}$ in. from the edge. Leave the threads long enough to pull. If you're lining the button, attach the lining to the material with the same stitches.

Pull the threads to gather the circle of material loosely into a cap. Then insert the button form. Pull the threads until the material is wrapped tightly and evenly around the form. If there's a pattern on the material, position it as you want it, and then tie off the threads and clip them short.

Gently push the material down into the center back of the button and around the teeth. You don't have to worry about hooking the material tightly over the teeth, because the material is already secure. Finish the button by snapping on the back plate.
—*Amy T. Yanagi, Millersville, MD*

MATCHING BUTTONS

I used to be frustrated when I tried to match a card of buttons to my fabric swatch, as I could never really lay the button on the fabric. Now I snip a 1-in. slit in my swatch and button the card of buttons onto the fabric.
—*Jeannie K. McCormic, Many, LA*

RESTORING PEARL BUTTONS

I inherited a lot of beautiful, old pearl buttons from my grandmothers. Most needed to be cleaned and polished. After removing the old thread, I rubbed the buttons between my fingers with a paste of baking soda and water.
—*Pearl Koning, South Holland, IL*

THRIFT SHOPS FOR NOTIONS

Thrift shops are a good potential source of inexpensive, hard-to-find fabrics and trims. You can sometimes find buttons, especially mother-of-pearl ones, on garments that cost less than you would pay for the buttons alone in retail stores. After I've taken the buttons or other trims off, I sew on replacements and donate the clothes back to the shop. Other hard-to-find notions to look for in thrift shops include necktie interfacings, bra underwires, fur trims, interesting belt buckles, and so on.
—*Susan Klement, Tucson, AZ*

KEEPING TRACK OF OLD BUTTONS

If I want to reuse the buttons on a worn-out garment, I cut off the strips of fabric with buttons still on them (cuffs, openings, etc.) and pin them together. It's a handy way to keep sets together while you store the buttons.

—*Jean Margolis, Sebastopol, CA*

DYEING YOUR OWN BUTTONS

If I can't find the colored buttons I want, I dye white, porous plastic buttons in Tintex or Rit dye (found in your local supermarket). Since each button takes color differently, I do two or three sets of buttons at once, so I have enough of the same shade. Stir the buttons in the dye bath and remove them when they are a shade darker than desired. Clean them thoroughly with soapy water, and then set the color by soaking them in white vinegar. The garment that sports your custom buttons should be washed in cool or lukewarm water to prevent the buttons from fading.

—*Mrs. Walter Neff, Muscoda, WA*

FELT BUTTONS

Felt buttons are lightweight even when they're large; they can be used for decoration, as well as for closures. To make them, you need felt, scissors, and two small bowls, one with very hot water and the other with ice water.

Cut the felt into squares the approximate size you wish the buttons to be. Dunk a square of felt into the hot water, into the ice water, and then into the hot water again. Between dunkings, squeeze the water out of the felted square and form it into a ball. Roll the ball between your palms with increasing pressure as it becomes round. Eventually, you'll be able to roll two or three balls of similar size at the same time. Set the balls aside to dry. One side may be slightly uneven, but you can use it for stitching through the felt.

—*Helen von Ammon, San Francisco, CA*

MAKING FABRIC CORDS

To make cords for loop and button enclosures, cut a bias strip of your fabric 2 in. wide by 5 in. long. Press it in half lengthwise, right sides together. Then pull out the top and bobbin threads on your sewing machine for about 8 in., and twist them together to form a single cord. Place the cord inside the crease, and keep it taut. Sew about ¼ in. from the fold, making sure to backstitch at both ends and being careful not to stitch over the threads inside the fold. Trim the seam allowance close, and then pull on the inside threads while rolling the fabric in and over itself. Once you have it started, it will slide easily. Cut the fabric cord to the desired length.

Twelve inches is about as long a fabric cord as you can make this way, but be sure the thread cord inside is longer than the fabric piece. You can make fancy shaped loops by inserting a sturdy wire into the cord and bending it as desired. —*Heather L. Taylor, Media, PA*

COVERED SNAPS

Covered snaps used to anchor internal facings can add an elegant, finished look to the inside of a garment. Often a snap holds a neck or front opening flat against the underlayer when the button or other closure lies too far from the edge to secure the opening fully. Nancy Nehring, who makes needle-lace buttons and fancy frog closures to adorn the clothes she sews, often uses covered snaps to help secure a garment's underlap or overlap. Because a snap can be located so near the edge, its metallic color may show on the outside of the garment and mar the overall effect. Covering the snaps with self-fabric or fabric in a matching color solves the problem.

For a covered snap, select a size 3 (13mm) or larger snap. Smaller snaps are difficult to cover and probably too small to support the weight of the opening or facing on an adult garment. To cover the snap, use a lightweight, tightly woven fabric; lining fabric or lightweight self-fabric works well.

For each snap, cut two circles of fabric twice the diameter of the snap or slightly smaller.

Start with the male, or protruding, half of the snap. With a single strand of thread, sew a running stitch about ⅛ in. from the outside edge of the fabric circle. Leave a 3-in. to 6-in. tail at each end of the thread. With a sharp instrument, work a hole in the center of the fabric circle. Nehring uses the point of her embroidery scissors to start the hole and an awl to enlarge it, trying not to cut or break the fabric threads. Push the hole in the fabric down over the bump in the center front of the snap, then pull the thread tails to gather the fabric around the back of the snap. Tie the thread tails at the back.

On the second circle of fabric, work a running stitch and center hole as for the first circle. Although it's not mandatory, Nehring works an eyelet stitch around the center hole to hold the hole open and reduce wear on the fabric with repeated use of the snap. To sew the eyelet stitch, bring a threaded needle through the fabric from the back ¹⁄₁₆ in. from the hole. Pass the needle and thread down through the hole, move ⅛ of the way around the circle, and come up again. Repeat around the hole, as shown in Fig. 131. If you choose not to work the eyelet stitch, you may want to seal the hole's edges with a liquid sealant such as Fray Check. To finish, hold the female, or indented, half of the snap with the center hole next to the hole in the fabric and pull up the thread tails; tie off as for the first half.

FIG. 131

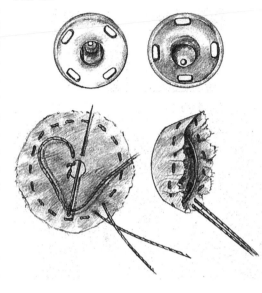

FIG. 132

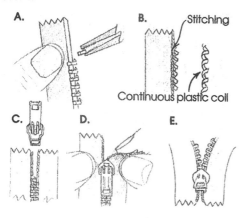

A.

B. Stitching

Continuous plastic coil

C.   D.   E.

FIG. 133

Shorten from
the top.

Stitch.

Shorten from
the bottom.

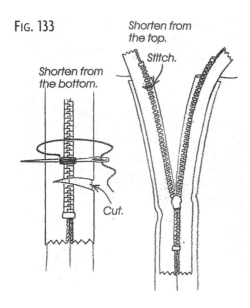

Cut.

To sew each half of the covered snap to the garment, work four stitches through each of the four holes near the snap's outer edge. Poke around the edge with the needle to locate the first hole; the others will be at 45° and 90° to it. Or, for a professional look, use a blanket stitch or other decorative stitch.

CONTINUOUS ZIPPERS

Continuous zippers come as tapes that can be cut to any length, which is convenient when you need an extra-long zipper for a comforter cover. You can buy zippers with metal or plastic teeth, or plastic coils. The zipper slide must be added to the tape and is not interchangeable between zipper types.

Before you sew the tape into a seam, you must remove the teeth from the seam allowances. Use a pair of needle-nose pliers to pull off teeth as shown in step A of Fig. 132. To remove a coil, cut down the center of the exposed coil (step B), then remove the broken curls with tweezers. Don't cut into the tape; it will fray.

Insert the tapes into the bottom of the slide as shown in step C. Grasp the tape ends securely and pull down on the slide. It sometimes helps to pull the tapes outward and tap the top of the slide to start it (step D).

If you separate the zipper completely, feed the tape ends into the top of the slide, and pull it up (step E).

INVISIBLE ZIPPER IN ANY COLOR WORKS

If an invisible zipper doesn't come in the color of your choice, just paint the zipper pull (the only part that actually shows). Model paints, available in hobby stores, as well as cheap nail polish easily overcoat the original color. To create a color to match your fabric, you may have to experiment. A pale pink over a pale blue makes a light lilac, deep green over black makes forest green, and blue over pink makes grape. Color the pull prior to installing the zipper in the garment. Cut a protective cover out of aluminum foil for the zipper and pull the tab through a small slit in the foil. Apply one layer of color at a time and allow it to dry before checking the match.
—*Dee DuMont, Bainbridge Island, WA*

SHORTENING A ZIPPER

To shorten a zipper from the bottom, first sew several stitches in one place over the teeth (by hand or by machine) at the desired length to serve as the new zipper stop. Then cut the zipper about ½ in. below it, as shown in Fig. 133. A zipper may also be shortened from the top, if the edge is going to be finished with a waistband or collar. Stitch in the zipper first, then sew several stitches over the teeth on each side of the zipper at the desired length, and cut.

LUBRICATING ZIPPER TEETH

Metal zippers open and close more easily when you lubricate the metal teeth with a paraffin wax such as Parowax, found in most housewares stores. Simply slide a bar of the household wax back and forth over the teeth on both sides of the opened zipper. The wax is transparent and will not wash off in the laundry.

—*Andrea Moore, Spokane, WA*

NEW LIFE FOR ELASTIC

When the elastic in a garment starts to wear out, I've found that you can revitalize it by basting elastic cord or thread into the old elasticized area. I simply pull up the ends after I've stitched all the way around, and tie them off at the tension I want. It really works!

—*Susan L. Weiner, Spring Hill, FL*

READY-MADE WAISTBAND ELASTIC

In desperate need of finishing a skirt, I cut the elastic waistband from the top of an old pair of panty hose. It was the perfect length and width, and it fit right into the casing on the skirt I was making. I have since tried just topstitching recycled waistbands in place with great results.

—*Jeanne Schimmel, Island Park, NY*

DOUBLE-FOLD BIAS STRIPS

Here's a way to make double-fold bias of any width and of any weight material. First cut the bias strip four times the desired finished width. Fold lengthwise in half and press, as shown in Fig. 134. Fold lengthwise in half again, with raw edges just short of the first fold. You now have double-fold tape with one fold going the wrong way. When you fold one half the right way, you'll find that it naturally folds just to the inside of the wrong way fold. Press again, and you have double-fold bias binding that's a hair narrower on one side. If you want very narrow binding, it is somewhat easier to cut the strip overly wide at first, and trim the raw edges after making the second fold.

—*Liisa Mannery, Seattle, WA*

BIAS-STRIP FOLDERS FROM THE KITCHEN

If you need a bias-strip folder in a different size than the bias-tape makers sold in notions catalogs, try a cake decorator's tube called a petal tube. Available in a variety of sizes anywhere decorating supplies are sold (a ⅜-in. tip cost me 69¢), these little metal cones have a flat slot opening at the narrow end into which you can slip a folded-in-half strip cut twice the width of the opening. You can pin the end coming from

FIG. 134

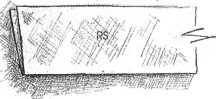
Fold bias strip lengthwise and press.

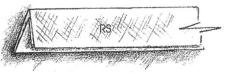
Fold and press lengthwise again, with raw edges just short of fold.

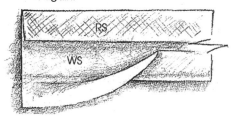
Unfold inside half of strip and make new fold in the opposite direction, just to the inside of the original wrong-way fold. Press again.

the tip of the tube to your ironing surface, then slide the tip ahead of the iron while you press the fold.

—*Cynthia Pool, Sunnyvale, CA*

KEEPING TRACK OF THE GRAIN

I purchase interfacings on sale in large quantities but often am left with pieces without the original straight edge. To guarantee a reference point for the grain line, I put a light grain line down the center of the piece with a yardstick and pencil before cutting into it.

—*Diane J. Whipple, Kent, WA*

FIG. 135

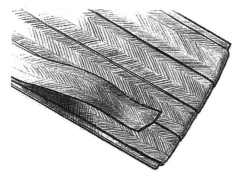

TWILL TAPE

Twill tape, a firmly woven tape that is used to stabilize seams and mark necklines, is available in black and white in various widths from ¼ to 1 in. It can be distinguished from other types of tape by its characteristic twill weave, as shown in Fig. 135. The twill tape that works best for tailoring is made of pure cotton, although the type available in most sewing stores is made of polyester.

PRESHRINKING SEAM TAPE

It's a good idea to preshrink seam tape, twill tape, etc., with your fabric. To avoid having to press it when it dries, wrap the damp tape around a large jar to dry.

—*Jan Jasper, New York, NY*

FAST PRESS FOR FLAT TRIMS

Here's a way to iron trims, tapes, flat cordings, ribbons, or strips of cloth quickly. First place a hot iron on a cotton pad over the trim to be ironed. Then apply light pressure to the iron and pull the trims from the back of the iron. Most wrinkles are removed easily.

—*Tenley Alaimo, Binghamton, NY*

STORING ELASTICS AND RIBBONS

Here's how to prevent elastic, cording, and laces from tangling together, while keeping them visible but protected from dust and direct light: Slide empty paper-towel and toilet-paper rolls over a wood or metal dowel from the hardware store. Suspend each end of the dowel beneath a shelf in your sewing room using wire, long-shaft cup hooks, or whatever is most appropriate for your shelving, so the dowel is removable. When the dowel is secure, wrap your notions around the tubes and roll them up. The farther toward the back of the shelf, the more protected the tubes will be.

—*Stacey Callahan, Toulouse, France*

STORING INTERFACING

Anyone who sews has to solve the problem of sorting and storing interfacings. I make an envelope for each type from the plastic instruction sheet. I fold the sheet and machine-sew the sides. Not only is this pocket, or envelope, quick and easy to make, but you'll know which interfacing is stored inside, and the instructions will always be there. It's great for storing all the scraps too.

—*Lynn Teichman, Lewisburg, PA*

FOR SMOOTHER COLLARS

When you're testing interfacings for collars and other details that need to fold or roll smoothly, be sure to try out different directions for the interfacing grain. Even if your outer fabric is on the straight grain, you can get some of the benefits of bias by fusing a bias-cut interfacing to it. In the same vein, you can get some of the qualities of knit fabrics into your wovens by using knit interfacings on the bias and both cross- and straight-grain directions on straight-grain wovens. You'll definitely notice the different effect of each choice.

—*Frederika Hausman, Naples, FL*

HANDY LEFTOVER FUSIBLES

I save all my odd bits of SofKnit fusible and put them to good use in the following ways: Thin strips of fusible can be used to stabilize zipper seam allowances, and a thin strip, cut on the nonstretch grain, can substitute for stay tape around the waist of a bias-cut skirt. Small curved pieces reinforce fabric areas that must be clipped, such as sleeve curves, princess lines, and portions of seam allowances that fray.

—*Keith Farmer, Newark, NJ*

THREAD

Many types of thread are composed of two or more strands of fiber twisted together to make a new, stronger strand. Cotton thread, for example, is usually either two-ply or three-ply, meaning that either two or three separately spun threads have been twisted to form it. To determine the number of plies in a thread, simply untwist a short length of the thread, as shown in Fig. 136. Two-ply cotton thread is not, as a rule, intended for garment construction, but high-quality brands will work beautifully on most lightweight fabrics.

Thread weight is often described with a pair of numbers separated by a slash, such as 60/2. The first number indicates the size of one separately spun strand, or ply, of the thread; smaller sizes are higher numbers, so size 60 is smaller than size 50. The second number indicates how

FIG. 136

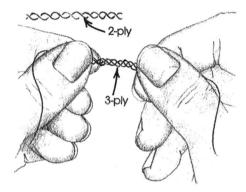

many plies have been twisted together to form the thread. There are two plies in both 60/2 and 50/2 thread, but the 50/2 thread will be stronger and thicker.

THREAD NAP
Doing all hand stitching with the nap of the thread down from the needle will result in fewer tangles and knots, less untwisting and abrasion, and a better appearance because the thread nap will react uniformly to light rays. However, it's not always easy to figure out how the nap goes on some threads.

You can test wool for direction of nap by drawing the strand up and down between thumb and forefinger. The beginning of the smooth pass is the end that should go in the needle, with the waste knot at the other end.

Unfortunately, sense of touch doesn't work on all fibers. Filaments—man-made or silkworm-made—aren't a problem, because they are single, continuous strands without nap, but other threads can be tricky. The best way I know to find the nap on these fibers is to compare two freshly cut ends of the thread. One end is always more rounded and more tightly twisted than the other, which tends to splay outward (Fig. 137). If the difference isn't obvious, gently blow on the two ends. The rounded end should enter the eye of the needle.
—*Bee Borssuck, Scottsdale, AZ*

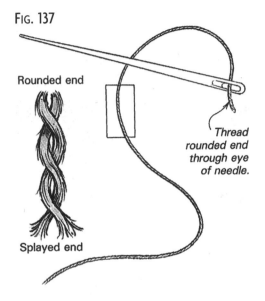

FIG. 137

Rounded end

Splayed end

Thread rounded end through eye of needle.

MULTIPURPOSE BOBBIN THREAD
I always keep a full bobbin of transparent thread handy for little sewing projects or alterations that require only a small amount of colored thread. I thread my machine needle with the proper color and pop in the transparent bobbin thread. No more winding bobbins partway.
—*Anna Maria Balzarini, Brewster, MA*

INVISIBLE THREAD
Had it not been for a sales clerk ranting about how awful invisible thread was, I would never have put it to the test, other than for the intended purpose. I found that a loose top tension is necessary to perfect straight sewing (#2 on my Elna). But my biggest suprise came when I tried a buttonhole on a scrap of silk. With no preparation, except the looser top tension, my very first buttonhole was perfect, with no puckers.
—*Shirley Hastings, Kamloops, British Columbia, Canada*

ALTERNATIVE HAND-SEWING THREADS
After years of being dissatisfied with conventional and specialty threads for hand sewing, which snag, snap, and twist, I have substituted No. 8 pearl cotton and embroidery floss for many of my finishing touches to garments. I

haven't found anything better for making French tacks and thread chains, or sewing snaps and buttons.

—*Martha McKeon, Sandy Hook, CT*

THREAD FOR HEAVY NYLON FABRIC

I had a hard time finding a workable combination of thread and machine needle for a recent project using Cordura (a heavy, coated nylon used for outerwear, duffel bags, and the like) until I tried nylon fishing-rod winding thread. Available at many sport and tackle stores, this multistrand thread worked much better than either heavy cotton/poly or monofilament thread, and I was able to use a standard 80/12 machine needle with the finest weight (size A) thread. A 950-yd. spool cost me less than $4. Cabela's carries black, white, and 23 colors, in three weights, and even has a metallic gold in size A.

—*Nancy Barr, Auke Bay, AK*

FUSIBLE THREAD

Fusible thread, blended from polyester and nylon, melts when ironed to provide a bond between layers of fabric. Sewing with fusible thread in the bobbin of a sewing machine, with regular thread for the top thread, allows you to fuse the bobbin side of the fabric to another layer. It's best to sew with a wide utility stitch, such as the one shown in Fig. 138, or a wide zigzag, because the more fusible thread that is exposed, the more secure the bond will be.

When it is used to apply binding to a quilt, fusible thread serves as a basting step that will hold the binding in place until it can be permanently stitched.

EASY BELT LOOPS

To make easy belt loops, cut about six strands of sewing thread 6 in. long for each loop. Place the strands under the presser foot of your sewing machine, and sew a zigzag stitch over them, being sure to catch them all.

—*Charlotte Pierce, Greensburg, KY*

NO-SLIP BELTS

Here's a great solution for belts that slip up and off your waistband in back: Back your belt with a strip of the rubberized fabric sold to make the feet of children's pajamas nonslip. This works whether it's the belt or the fabric that's slippery. Some brands of this fabric ravel, so if you're making a belt, machine-sew the strips on with a wide, long satin stitch; for ready-to-wear belts, whipstitch the strips on by hand or use glue. In either case, douse the edges of the strips with a no-fray liquid.

—*Virginia Cavanagh, San Jose, CA*

FIG. 138

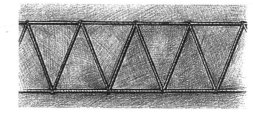

INDEX

Look for these and other *Threads* books at your local bookstore or sewing retailer.

For a catalog of the complete line of *Threads* books and videos, write to The Taunton Press, PO Box 5506, Newtown, CT 06470-5506. Or call (800) 888-8286.